HOW TO WIN YOUR SCHOOL APPEAL

Getting your child into the school of your choice

SECOND EDITION

BEN ROONEY

A & C BLACK • LONDON

Second edition 2007
First published 2005
A & C Black Publishers Ltd
38 Soho Square
London W1D 3HB
www.acblack.com

© 2005, 2007 Ben Rooney

ISBN 978-0-7136-8236-6

This book is produced using paper that is made
from wood grown in managed, sustainable forests.
It is natural, renewable and recyclable. The logging and
manufacturing processes conform to the environmental
regulations of the country of origin.

Printed in Great Britain by
Caligraving Ltd, Thetford, Norfolk

Contents

Introduction

If you are reading this book, then the chances are you have recently received a bitter blow. Your child has not been offered a place at the school of your choice. For most parents this is a terrible time, a time of great worry. What to do now? Where will my child go to school? Some of you may be thinking of moving home; others may be resigned to your fate.

But there is another chance: take your case to appeal. Appeal panels, which are completely independent of schools and local education authorities, have the power to consider your application, review any evidence you may provide, speak to any witnesses you may wish to bring, and make a ruling on it. And what they decide, goes. If they agree that your child should go to the school, then he or she will – whether or not the school or the Local Authority agrees. Appeal panels have a lot of power, a lot of independence and have shown, time and time again, that they are not afraid to use it.

However, many parents find the whole process of appealing both intimidating and confusing. They are worried about what to expect, about how to prepare a case, about how and where they can get information. And they have other worries, too: how long will it take; do they have a good case; what *is* a good case; where can they find out more?

Such concerns are not without foundation. Appeal-panel members will tell you that they go out of their way to make the whole process as 'parent-friendly' as they can. And many do. But that does not take away the fact that it is a difficult process. You are in a room, confronted by a group of strangers about whom you know very little. You are pitted against either the school, or the Local Authority, or sometimes both. Everyone else in that room will have had specialist training for their role, but no one else present has as much to lose as you do. If they make a mistake, it doesn't affect them personally. If you make a mistake, if you don't give it your best shot, well, you don't get another chance. So with all that going on in your head you have to sit there and make a rational, well-constructed argument about one of the most precious things in your life – your child. That is tough.

Even before you get into the room, there is the worry of the paper-work. How do you find out about the appeal process? The amount of information available to parents on how to go about making an appeal has been extremely limited. Every parent is supposed to be sent advice, but all too often that advice is perfunctory at best, and in some cases little more than a single side of paper. Other parents may get nothing at all.

Despite all of the above, more and more parents are putting themselves through the appeal process; more and more parents refuse to be cowed and intimidated. During the last year for which the government released figures (2004/05) just over 80,000 appeals were lodged; that is getting on for one appeal per 15 places offered. And although the total number of appeals lodged by parents has gone down from a peak in 2002/03, so too has the number of children applying to schools. But there is one thing that has remained reasonably consistent – your chance of success. Slightly more than two out of three appeals will fail, and the figures are broadly speaking the same for primary school appeals as for secondary.

This book was written to help parents. It isn't an 'appeals for the stupid' guide or a 'make that sale' book; nor does it offer ten easy steps to getting the right school place for your child. There are no shortcuts in here, no magic formulae that will guarantee you success. However, it is based on a wealth of experience and advice – both personal and that of appeal-panel members, parents, education officials and clerks, all of whom have direct experience of appeals, and some of whom have attended hundreds. It is a guide to help you understand how the process works, how to prepare your appeal, the questions to ask, the places to go to find out information. It will help you draw up your appeal, help you plan a strategy, and give you advice on tactics that work – and some that don't. Throughout the book are case studies to show success, or in some instances, failure. All of the case studies are anonymous; in some, two or more may have been amalgamated to form a single case. But they are all drawn from real cases that appeared before panels.

Many parents may be daunted by the length of the book, or by how complicated it all appears. You may be worried that you couldn't possibly do all the things the book says; you haven't the time, or the ability. But ask yourself this. How much do you want your child to get into that particular school? If your answer is not very much, then a quick flip through these pages may be enough to pick up a few basic tips which will help you. But if, like many, many parents, you are faced with the choice of sending your child to an unsuitable school – one about which you are very worried, one that troubles you – then ask yourself how much time is too much? What price your child's future?

This book is quite openly and unashamedly on your side. It sounds a cruel and selfish thing to say, but you may well be in competition with fellow parents to win a place at your chosen school. When there are only a limited number of places available, if another child gets in, it makes it harder for your child. So this book is not about making the admission system fairer, or more accessible. It is not about the rights and wrongs of the appeal system, or about championing anything. It is about stacking the pack just a little bit more in your favour so that when you enter that room to fight for your child's future, you hold some of the trump cards.

Although many different people contributed to these pages, they all agreed on one essential message: if you want to win your appeal, you must prepare for it. You must know the facts of the case, you must have thought about the points you want to make, and you must be aware of the arguments the other side will make. Without a doubt, the most common mistake that parents make in school appeals is to fail to ask the right questions – and in many, many cases they fail to ask any questions at all. All too often parents simply take what the school or the Local Authority says at face value and don't challenge it. That is half the battle lost before you have even started.

In my own case, our appeal hinged around distance to school. We were able to show that the school's system was flawed, and that the error margin in the system was greater than the distance between our unsuccessful application and the nearest successful one. As it turned out in the meeting, the admission authority produced a map showing the various houses (a map that they had not previously circulated). It played into our hands, as they had incorrectly identified the two successful houses, although they had correctly identified ours. We were able to show that the admission authority had not correctly applied their admission criteria – or, to be more precise, on balance of probability the panel could not be confident that they had – and our appeal was upheld. In our authority there were 34 appeals lodged; only three others were upheld.

Our case was just one of thousands heard that year. When we first read the case against our son, our appeal seemed unwinnable. After all, if your house is too far away, then it is too far away. But by really looking into the facts, checking them carefully, investigating the procedures that the school had adopted, it was quickly clear that far from being unwinnable, we had in fact been denied a place that was ours.

Although every situation is different, there are lessons to be learned from our case – and from thousands of others. Don't accept the case presented against you without being certain that the facts are correct. Use this book to help you uncover the truth, ask the right questions, look closely at the case against you, and prepare the very best case you can to win a place for your child at the school of your choice.

Notes: This is the second edition of *How to Win Your School Appeal*, and reflects changes made to the law in 2005 and 2006. One of the most tangible reforms has been a change in the role of what were Local Education Authorities (LEAs), to a broader remit encompassing other, non-education functions. This has led to some confusion, since the title of Local Education Authority has been largely replaced by the more general term, Local Authority. However, the existing codes of practice were published before the changes; where the codes are quoted directly, the term LEA will be used.

This year is likely to be the last in which admissions are organised under the old admission code: substantial changes to admissions and appeals are due to come into effect from September 2007. At the time of writing, these revisions were still out for consultation; some of the proposals are listed at Appendix 1.

This book quotes throughout from the two statutory documents on school admissions and admission appeals. These are: *The School Admissions Code of Practice*; and *The School Admission Appeals Code of Practice*. Details of how to obtain copies are given on pp. 36–7.

Acknowledgements

My thanks to everyone who shared their experiences and advice on school appeals, including parents, clerks, appeal-panel members and school governors. I hope that your collected wisdom and experience – which between you all must have been gained from thousands of appeals – has been faithfully distilled.

I would like to thank Katie Taylor and Jonathan Glasspool at A&C Black for their support during the project, Hilary Lissenden for her proof-reading, and my agent Robert Dudley for fighting my corner and coming up trumps.

Thanks also to the Commission for Local Administration in England for allowing the use of their material, and to the Department for Education and Skills for granting copyright permission.

I would like to thank my son, Hugo, without whom this project would never have been conceived, and because of whom we fought, and won, our case.

But above all I would like to thank my darling wife Jenny, for putting up with my long hours at the keyboard, providing limitless encouragement and practical advice, and above all, love.

Ben Rooney
January 2007
http://www.winyourschoolappeal.co.uk

CHAPTER 1

The admission process

Who determines which children are admitted? Who or what is an
'admission authority'? Who is a parent? How are selections
made? On what grounds can an admission authority turn down a
child? Why didn't my child get a place? What criteria are used?
Commonly used criteria. Children with special educational needs
or disabilities. Waiting lists

Who determines which children are admitted?

Every maintained school in the country has an admission authority
that decides who gets into that school and who must be turned away.
The authority will consider all the applications to the school. If there
are more places available at the school than there were applications,
then every child who applied will get a place. If more children apply
than there are places available, then the authority will have to decide
which children are admitted and which ones are turned down by
applying its published admission criteria – the list of criteria that says
who gets priority.

   If there are places at your chosen school (and, in the case of selective schools, your child qualifies for a place), the admission authority
must offer one. Admission authorities cannot reserve places, for
example in the expectation that there may be later applications from
families moving into a catchment area. (There may be special considerations for families of Service personnel, which will be covered later.)

Who or what is an 'admission authority'?

As with so much in education, there is no single answer to this.
Different schools do things differently according to whether the
school is a Community school, a Foundation school, a Voluntary
Controlled (VC) school or a Voluntary Aided (VA) school. (Appeals to
Special Schools are not considered in this book.)

   Broadly speaking, Voluntary schools – either Aided or Controlled –
are likely to be schools of a religious nature. Foundation schools are

self-governing schools with a higher level of independence from the Local Authority than other categories (they used to be referred to as Grant Maintained schools). Community schools are Local Authority-run (and used to be known as County schools). There are more Community schools than there are schools in any other category.

The distinction affects who has control over the school's admissions, and to a lesser extent, how the appeal process is run.

Type of school	Who sets the admission criteria?
Community	*Local Authority* *(May be delegated to the school in some cases)*
Foundation	*School governing body*
Voluntary Aided	*School governing body*
Voluntary Controlled	*Local Authority* *(May be delegated to the school in some cases)*

Things to consider

There are some practical considerations in appealing to an independent appeal panel for a Foundation or VA school, and appealing to one for a Community or VC school. If you appeal to a panel conducted on behalf of the Local Authority, there are two points to keep in mind:

- The Local Authority is likely to have a huge amount of experience in running appeals. They may well have a dedicated appeal officer and will certainly have access to a legal team that is extremely well versed in education law. Your appeal therefore must be especially well prepared.
- An appeal against a Local Authority decision is likely to cover not only your appeal against a decision not to offer your child a place at your chosen school, but may well in effect be an appeal against the offer at the allocated school. Although the appeal panel is strictly speaking only empowered to consider the first aspect, you should keep in mind that you may in effect be fighting 'on two fronts'.

By contrast, an appeal against a VA or Foundation school will be made to a panel that has been appointed by the school. It is likely that a school governor will run the case for the school, and while they may not have as much experience at preparing and running cases as a Local Authority official, they may very well have a better working knowledge of the school.

Who is a parent?

The law places a lot of emphasis on parental rights and a parent's right to choose, but that rather presupposes that we know who the parents are. In most cases it is obvious, but the question 'Who *are* a pupil's parents?' is not always as straightforward as it sounds.

Section 576 of the Education Act 1996 defines 'parent' to include:

- all natural parents, whether they are married or not; and
- any person who, although not a natural parent, has *parental responsibility* for a child or young person; and
- any person who, although not a natural parent, *has care* of a child or young person.

Having *parental responsibility* means assuming all the rights, duties, powers, responsibilities and authority that a parent of a child has by law. People other than a child's natural parents can acquire parental responsibility through:

- being granted a residence order;
- being appointed a guardian;
- being named in an emergency protection order (although parental responsibility in such a case is limited to taking reasonable steps to safeguard or promote the child's welfare); or
- adopting a child.

In addition, a local authority can acquire parental responsibility if it is named in the care order for a child, although any person who is a parent or guardian retains parental responsibility and may exercise it providing their actions are not incompatible with the care order. While the care order is in force, the local authority can refuse contact with the parent and does not have to seek parental consent. Children can also be 'accommodated', whereby there is a joint arrangement between the parents and the local authority that the latter will look after the child. This does not, however, involve a court order and the parents can withdraw from the arrangement if they choose to do so.

The parental responsibility of one party does not stop simply because another person is also given it. So, in some cases several people may be regarded, for the purposes of education law, as being the 'parent' of a child.

Having *care of* a child or young person means that a person with whom the child lives, and who looks after the child, irrespective of what their relationship is with the child, is considered to be a parent in education law.

Recent legislation has given 'looked-after children' priority in applications, a view being reflected in the rulings of the Office of the Schools Adjudicator – the body responsible for overseeing school admissions.

So you do not have to be the biological or even step, or foster, parent of a child to be able to lodge an appeal on his or her behalf.

How are selections made?

The admission process is a trying time for all parties concerned. Parents are naturally worried, the children are anxious to go to their chosen school, and admission authorities work hard to ensure that as many children as possible get to attend the school of their choice. But it is inevitable that many children and parents will be disappointed. For the simple truth is that good schools get many more applications than they can reasonably accept, so that many children will have to be turned down.

Historically the admission process has been a fraught one. Until the 2005/6 admission round, things were very confusing for parents, children and schools. Rules and regulations developed in a haphazard way, with different admission authorities having different application forms, setting different closing dates for submissions and sending out offers on different days. Furthermore, each authority made its own decision independent of every other, so it was possible for one child to have two, three or even more offers of places, while your child had none. Not only was this extremely distressing for parents and children, it was also wildly inefficient. Many schools did not know how many children would be starting school until the first day of term, as parents kept their options open right until the last minute.

Changes introduced in 2005, the 'unified admission' procedures, mean that parents fill in a standard application form for all schools, regardless of whether they are Community, VA, VC or Foundation schools. Parents list schools in order of preference. There is a single closing date by which the form must be returned to the Local Authority, and forms arriving after the closing date will be treated as late applications.

For many schools the single application form gives them all they need, but for some – mainly schools of a religious character – the form does not provide enough information, such as evidence of religious belief. These schools are allowed to require parents to complete a supplementary application form, but this form may not request information over and above that needed for schools to reasonably apply their published admission criteria.

CASE STUDY

A school had an admission number of 170. The school told the Local Authority, which was the admission authority, that it had received 207 applications and would like to accept all of them. The Local Authority agreed that all 207 children could be admitted.

But the Headteacher then refused to admit one applicant. This was a boy who had two older brothers at the school and should have had priority for that reason. However, because of an earlier alleged incident involving one of the older boys, and because of the parents' contact with the school over other matters, relations between the Headteacher and parents had become acrimonious. The younger boy was the only child refused a place.

The parents appealed, with the following outcome. The admission authority had agreed to accept 207 children, but only 206 had been admitted. Therefore, the admission authority had a duty to admit the child. The Headteacher, acting on behalf of the admission authority, had acted inappropriately in refusing a place.

Completed forms are returned to the Local Authority, which gathers in every application for every school in its area. For some schools (VC and Community schools) the Local Authority is the admission authority and will be responsible for deciding which children to admit; for others (VA and Foundation schools) it plays no role in deciding which children get a place but simply passes over to each school a list of every child that applied there. The governing bodies of these schools will then apply their own admission criteria to the names on the list.

All the admission authorities then return to the Local Authority a list of children to whom they are prepared to make offers, in order of priority. The Local Authority takes all those returns and starts the complicated process of making the individual offers.

The unified admission system is designed to give each child a place at his or her highest preference school. So, for example, if a child applies to three schools and is offered places at the second and third preference school but not at the first, the Local Authority will offer the child a place at his or her second preference school, but not the third.

The government has given each Local Authority a lot of choice as to how it will run its system, as long as it achieves the overall objective of allowing parents to rank schools, and ensuring that children are given a single offer at their highest ranked school. For instance, the clearing Local Authority may require admission authorities to make decisions on first preference applicants ahead of others, and only move onto second preference applicants once those children have been allocated places.

Whatever system is used, it must adhere to the same basic rules. The Local Authority must ensure that the form enables parents to:

- express their preferences, i.e. name the schools to which they are applying;
- give the reasons for applying to their preferred schools; and
- rank those preferences.

All preferences must be ranked, even if admission authorities in the area do not use a ranking system as part of their individual admission arrangements. The information about where in the ranking a parent placed a particular school is only passed on to a school if its admission criteria gives priority to children who rank it first. Other admission authorities are not told, for fear that it might wrongly become a factor in deciding which children to admit.

There will be a few unfortunate cases where no place is available at any of the chosen schools. In such instances the Local Authority is under an obligation to provide a place at a maintained school for every child that applies, at the closest school to the parents' address that has available places.

A parent may appeal to any school to which they have applied without success. If a parent is unsuccessful in securing an offer at their first priority school, but is offered a place at their second or third, this in no way reduces their right of appeal.

Things to consider
- If any school turns you down, you have a right of appeal to an independent appeal panel – even if you are offered a place at another school.
- Some admission authorities have, as a published criterion, preference given to children who rank the school as a first preference. Only these schools may use your ranking to help decide who is offered a place. Schools that do not specifically mention parental ranking as a published admission criterion should not be told where in the ranking you placed the school.

On what grounds can an admission authority turn down a child?

> **LEGAL POINT**
> *Every maintained school in England and Wales is obliged by law to publish its admission criteria and the number of children it will admit each year. Admission authorities are under a legal duty (Section 86(2) of the School and Standards Framework Act 1998, as amended by the Education Act 2002) to comply with parental preference except in very limited circumstances.*

Schools must take your child unless they have a very good reason not to. The law only allows five such reasons:

1 Where to admit the child would 'prejudice the provision of efficient education or the efficient use of resources'. Local Authorities and governing bodies may not refuse to admit children to any year group in which pupils are normally admitted to the school on these grounds, unless the number of preferences or applications for places in that relevant year group exceeds the school's admission number (see also pp. 83–4). Prejudice may arise by reason of measures that would be required to be taken to comply with the limit on infant class sizes (this will be covered in Chapter 8).

2 Where the school is wholly selective by high ability or by aptitude, and admission of the pupil would be incompatible with such selection under the admission arrangements. (Partially selective schools, and those which operate banding, must admit up to their published admission numbers.) Schools that are partially selective – sometimes referred to as 'bilateral schools' or as having 'grammar school streams' – may not keep selective places empty. Only schools that are wholly selective by high academic ability or by aptitude, and those admitting to their sixth form by reference to academic ability, can keep places empty if they do not have sufficient applicants of the required standard (see Chapter 8).

3 Where the child has been permanently excluded from two or more schools, and at least one of the exclusions took place after 1 September 1997. The requirement to comply with parental preference is disapplied for two years after the second exclusion. However, a child is not to be taken as having been permanently excluded for these purposes where: the exclusion took place before the child reached compulsory school age; the pupil was reinstated following exclusion; or a governing body reviewing the decision to permanently exclude a pupil, or an appeal panel hearing an appeal, decided it would have been appropriate for them to direct that the pupil be reinstated had they considered it practical for them to do so in the circumstances. A permanent exclusion is regarded as taking effect from the first school day the Headteacher has told the pupil not to attend the school.

4 Where state-maintained boarding schools have set separate admission numbers for day pupils and boarding pupils, and have more applicants for one or other category than places available – even though places may be available in the other category.

5 Where another place has been offered, as identified under coordinated arrangements.

Why didn't my child get a place?

Unless your child falls into one of the above five categories, the reason he or she did not get a place was because the school to which you applied gave preference to other children with a greater claim to a place according to the published admission criteria. In addition, the admission authority felt that to admit more children would 'prejudice the provision of efficient education and the efficient use of resources'. In ordinary language, other children were given higher priority. By the time they considered your child, the school was full; to take more children would have meant that the education of the children already at the school would suffer.

What criteria are used?

Each admission authority can decide on its own admission criteria, and the law is very flexible in allowing a wide range of these. There are no fixed criteria and the fact that an admission authority chooses not to adopt one or other, even if it is a very common one, is not grounds for an appeal. However, the School Admissions Code of Practice gives some general guidelines on the criteria (see panel).

LEGAL POINT

Admission authorities have discretion, which they must exercise reasonably, to determine their own oversubscription criteria, provided these criteria are objective, clear, fair, compatible with admissions and equal opportunities legislation, have been decided with regard to any relevant advice from the local Admission Forum, and have been subject to the consultation which the 1998 Act (as amended by the 2002 Act) requires. Admission authorities should consider how best to monitor school admission applications, refusals

> of places, and admission appeals to ensure that the admission process is fair and offers equal opportunities to all pupils. Schools and LEAs have a duty to promote racial equality under the Race Relations Act 1976 (as amended by the Race Relations (Amendment) Act 2000), and need to bear this in mind when deciding their over-subscription criteria. The criteria should be, as far as possible, inclusive of all elements in the school's local community.
> *School Admissions Code of Practice, Paragraph 3.4*

Not only must an admission authority decide on the admission criteria, it must also decide in which order to apply them. There are no limits on how many criteria an admission authority may apply; however, it must be very careful in drafting the exact wording of the criteria, for they should not be open to any interpretation.

Commonly used criteria

Many of the criteria that an admission authority will apply are not controversial and not open to interpretation. For example, many secondary schools will use 'feeder primaries', giving priority to children attending named schools at the time of application. This is a pass-or-fail test: either your child was in attendance at the time of application, or they were not.

The government has made it clear that it wishes 'looked-after children' – that is, children living in care or with foster families – to be given priority in applications.

However, there are many other criteria that are seemingly cut and dried, but are in fact open to interpretation. From an appeal point of view, the more room for interpretation there is, the better. If you can interpret the rules in such a way as to benefit your application, then that will go a long way towards helping you win your appeal. Some of the common problem areas include:

Sibling links
Many admission authorities recognise that a large number of parents want all their children to go to the same school, for very obvious reasons of transport and administration – to say nothing of the cost of school uniform. So a great many will give priority to parents applying to a school who already have a child there. This is commonly known as the 'sibling rule'.

Admission authorities applying the sibling rule will also need to define what constitutes a sibling. The dictionary definition of a blood link is considered by many to be too narrow, so authorities frequently widen it to include not only true siblings, but also half brothers or sisters, step brothers or sisters, and children of cohabiting partners. Foster children are sometimes included, although not universally.

Furthermore the published criteria need to make it clear *when* they require the sibling to attend, in order to be relevant. Some admission authorities say the sibling must be in attendance at the time of application; others at the time at which your child will be admitted. Some merely say that a sibling must have attended at some time.

There is a very common misconception that the sibling rule has some special place in law. It does not. Just because an admission authority chooses not to adopt the sibling rule, this does not in itself form the basis of an appeal. It may well be a factor to bring to the attention of the appeal panel, but there are admission authorities that do not give priority to siblings.

Indeed, this has been tested in the courts and there is case law on the subject (LB of Hounslow v Admissions Appeal Panel, 14 February 2002). Hounslow Local Authority operated a system of priority, or catchment, areas for its primary schools, whereby those living in the defined area were given priority. Three children who had brothers or sisters already at the school lived outside the priority area and were not allocated a place. The parents appealed, saying that it was unreasonable for the Local Authority not to allocate them a place: in return the Local Authority gave class-size prejudice as the reason why the parents' appeal should not be allowed. The appeal panel allowed the appeal on the basis that it was unreasonable not to give first priority to siblings.

But it did not stop there. The Local Authority vehemently disagreed with the appeal panel's ruling and sought a judicial review. Had the case been allowed to stand, the whole structure of the Local Authority's admission policy would have been undermined.

At the judicial appeal the judge ruled in the Local Authority's favour, overturning the decision that the appeal panel had made. The judge felt that there was no legal requirement for an admission authority to give absolute priority to siblings when deciding on criteria for allocating places in an oversubscribed school.

CASE STUDY

Ms D applied to a secondary school for a place for her younger daughter. Her elder daughter was at the school at the time of the application, but was to leave the school the term before the younger daughter joined. The admission authority operated the sibling rule that specified, 'Priority will be given to applicants who have a sibling attending the school.' Ms D was denied a place on the grounds that her elder daughter would not be in attendance when her younger daughter started, so she was not a priority applicant. She appealed against the decision. The panel agreed that the criterion was ambiguous: had the admission authority intended to operate a policy requiring the sibling to be at the school at the time of admission, then it should have stated this clearly. As the rule stood, it was unclear, and so the panel felt it was not unreasonable to interpret the regulation in the way Ms D had. The second daughter was awarded a place; furthermore the admission authority changed its policy to end the ambiguity.

Things to consider
- Do you have a child already attending the school?
- If so, and if your other child is denied a place although the school operates a sibling rule, then you almost certainly have a case.
- Check to see exactly what the sibling rule is, and when the sibling has to be at the school in order for you to apply. Many criteria are not that carefully phrased so there may be some element of doubt if, for example, your other child has left the school before the second one starts. If the criteria do not state that the sibling has to be in attendance when the second child starts, that could give you grounds for an appeal.

Special medical needs
Another very common priority is children who have a particular and pressing medical condition. There are many parents who claim that their child has a chronic though not severe medical condition (such as asthma) that necessitates their attendance at a certain school. In almost all cases this is insufficient grounds for an appeal.

To be successful you will need to show not only that your child has a particular medical condition, but also that this is of such a nature as to require special consideration; furthermore, that the school to which you are applying has a particular expertise, facility, design, experience, etc. to deal with that condition. The fact that your child suffers from asthma or any other relatively minor condition is not likely, of itself, to be sufficient grounds to win an appeal.

That being said, if your child does suffer from any long-term medical condition then do mention it at the time of application, even if the admission authority does not give priority to applicants with a medical condition. Admission authorities can only make their decisions on the information provided to them. Independent appeal panels may very well take chronic medical conditions into consideration even if they do not form part of the published admission criteria.

If you are going to claim priority under a medical condition, you must have evidence to support it. It is highly unlikely that your claim will be accepted without it.

CASE STUDY

Mr and Mrs S applied to a primary school for a place for their son. Priority was given to children with a medical condition, but because the parents had misunderstood the form they failed to mention on their application that their son was disabled and walked with the aid of crutches. The school to which they were granted a place was in a Victorian building with many steps, on numerous levels and on more than one floor. The school to which they were applying was a modern school on a single level.

The panel awarded a place to Mr and Mrs S but criticised them for failing to mention their son's special case at the time of application.

If your child has special educational needs then this will be covered later.

Distance

An almost universal tie-breaker. Children have been denied places while others in the same street, even neighbours, have been successful based entirely on distance measurements. Almost all admission authorities will have as part of their admission criteria something along the lines of: 'Where in any of the criteria, there are fewer places available than there are applicants of equal priority, places will be allocated with reference to the proximity of the child's home to the school, with those living nearest the school having first priority.'

What is seemingly a fairly straightforward rule is actually open to a wide range of interpretation that can be used to good effect for an appeal.

The first is the obvious point about what constitutes a home address. For most children this is not an issue: a child's home address is the address at which they live. But if you are divorced or separated, or never married and maintain two households, then your child may well spend equal – or if not equal, then significant – time at more than one address. Check from which address the school has measured.

In order to be successful you will need to produce evidence that your child lives there for at least part of the time. Such evidence could include any official post that mentions your child, such as your child being registered at that address with a doctor or dentist, or the address being used by your child's school. Increasingly, Local Authorities require proof of address to be submitted with applications. Admission authorities look extremely unfavourably on parents who try to cheat the system by renting houses inside catchment areas but not living there, or using other, similar tricks: such cheating is increasingly common and admission authorities *do* check. Where evidence of cheating is uncovered it is up to each admission authority to decide what steps to take. If they find out after places have been awarded, it is unlikely that a place, once offered, will be withdrawn – for that would be to punish the child. However, the admission authority may disregard the child if, for example, a sibling applies for a place and the authority uses a sibling link to determine priority. If the fraud is discovered before places are offered, then any priority ascribed to catchment is likely to be ignored and the application treated on its other merits.

Measuring the distance opens up all manner of issues. The two most common areas used successfully in appeals are how the distance was measured, and what was measured. Some admission authorities specify the distance to the school in a straight line (sometimes called 'as the crow flies'). Others may specify: by the shortest recognised walking route; by simple road measurement; or by public transport. There is some confusion, compounded by the official government advice, on whether admission authorities should use recognised routes or straight-line distance. The School Admissions Code of Practice says, 'Some admission authorities have been criticised by the Local Government Ombudsman for using methods which did not take into account the shortest walking distance.' However, there is nothing intrinsically right about shortest walking distance: for example, a rural secondary drawing children from miles distant would be unlikely to use shortest walking distance as a criteria. Nonetheless, such ambiguity can be used to your advantage. If the admission criteria do not specify how distance is to be measured, look and see if there are routes to the school that would be shorter.

Things to consider
- If the admission authority does not specify how it defines proximity to the school, it may be possible that your house is closer than that of another, successful, applicant. Check this carefully. If the authority specifies the shortest walking distance, make sure it *is* the shortest. Is it a safe route? If the suggested route doesn't have lighting, or a pavement, or is down unsafe alleyways and you can show a reasonable alternative that is safer, then you may have a case.
- Has the admission authority defined which points it measures? Cases have hinged on from which school gate the distance is

measured. If you are applying to an urban school with a small catchment area, this could be significant.

> **CASE STUDY**
> Mr G was denied a place for his child at a VA primary school. The school's governing body (the admission authority) said that their home was too far away. However, Mr G was able to show that there was a shorter, lit, and paved route to the school than that which the school had suggested. Furthermore, children who had been offered places walked past his house on the way to school. Mr G's appeal was successful.

Where the admission criteria specify distance 'as the crow flies', mistakes do occur in measuring distance. Many Local Authorities use commercial geographic mapping systems that allow them to identify addresses precisely and calculate the distance between them. These systems have a very high level of accuracy and you are unlikely to be able to challenge the measurement as long as the authority has correctly identified your address. (Check that it has: one appeal was won because the admission authority believed the applicant to reside in a particular house, when in fact they lived somewhere quite different.) However, many smaller admission authorities still rely on measuring distances on a map, despite government advice specifically criticising such techniques. 'Some admission authorities have been criticised by the Local Government Ombudsman for using methods which ... were poor at ensuring accuracy, for example using a ruler on a map.' (School Admissions Code of Practice, paragraph 3.6)

Some admission authorities use web-based systems to identify addresses, plot these on a map and then measure the distance on the map. This is a method that is open to error. Let's see how:

Identifying the parent's address: Most free web-based systems are based on postcodes. However, your postcode does not always uniquely identify your house; you can share it with anything up to 15 other addresses. What web-based map systems (such as multimap.com, streetmap.co.uk, etc.) do is to use a system that plots the estimated centre of the postcode, not your house. This can be very important, as the centre of your postcode area could be quite far away – far enough to introduce significant error in the measurement.

Schools in an urban area have a particular issue with multiple appeals from residents in tower blocks. Unfortunately there is no satisfactory way of dealing with such cases. Typically, priority will be given to those living closest to the recognised entrance or exit, in other words those on lower floors. The inherent injustice is clear.

CASE STUDY

Mr and Mrs R appealed against a Foundation secondary school that had turned down their son on the grounds that the distance to their house was 4mm further as the crow flies than that of a successful applicant. They were able to show a number of errors in the measuring system, including the use of a postcode-based system which they could prove was unable to locate the school accurately. They were able to show that the margin of error in the system was at least equal to 4mm. The appeal panel was not satisfied that the school had demonstrated that they lived further away than successful applicants, and the appeal was upheld.

Measuring distance: Admission authorities that persist in using map-based systems often fail to appreciate the inherent problems in maps. Many claim, for example, to measure from a defined point at the school to the front entrance of the parent's property. Unfortunately such accuracy is almost totally impossible using a 1:50,000 scale map, and only rarely possible using a 1:25,000 scale map (the two most commonly available Ordnance Survey maps). On a 1:25,000 scale map – the more accurate of the two – a front door would be represented by a line on the map narrower than a human hair.

Furthermore, even assuming an error margin in measuring of only 0.5%, over a distance of 300mm that equates to an error of 1.5mm. Admission authorities have rejected applicants who were 1mm further distant than successful applicants.

Things to consider
- Are you sure that the school has correctly identified your house?
- Are you sure that the school has correctly measured the distance (have you checked it)?
- Are there applicants living further away from you who were successful? If so, you have a very strong case.

Faith schools

Many parents, even those not of a strongly held religious conviction, are keen to send their children to 'church schools' and other single-faith schools. Historically these schools have performed well in national tests and frequently dominate the top half of the school league tables.

Many other parents strongly value the religious teachings of such schools, which tend to give them a very strong ethos and culture. For whatever reason, such schools are often heavily oversubscribed and appeals are frequent.

LEGAL POINT

Schools designated by the Department [for Education and Skills] as having a religious character may give preference in their admission arrangements to members of a particular faith or denomination (as may be required by their Trust Deed), providing this does not conflict with other legislation, such as race relations legislation. Where they do, their admission arrangements should make clear whether a statement of religious affiliation or commitment would be sufficient; whether it is to be 'tested' for admission purposes and if so, how; and what, if any, references would be required from the family's priest, Minister or other religious leader and how they will be used to decide on the application.

School Admissions Code of Practice, paragraph 3.9

Faith schools used to be allowed to reserve places for children of that faith, and could hold empty places. However, this practice has now been stopped and faith schools must offer places if they have them.

Although the *School Admissions Code of Practice* proscribed interviewing parents and/or children to determine religious faith, a London Catholic school won its court case to retain interviews.

The Judge ruled that while admission authorities were required to 'have regard' to the Code, this did not mean that there had to be 'slavish obedience or deference' to it on every occasion.

The effect of this ruling is that religious schools can, despite the *Code of Practice*, hold interviews; however, the circumstances under which they may do so are very limited. At the time of writing, the government has said that it will consider the Judge's ruling. It is possible that legislation may be brought in to address this issue.

Testing of religious faith is a very complex area and such tests must comply with the general requirements of all admission criteria (they must be clearly defined and objectively assessable). This can be very difficult. If you are denied a place at a faith school on the grounds that you failed to demonstrate sufficient religious commitment, then examine very closely the terms of the 'test'. It must be as it is stated, and not how the admission authority interprets it. For example, a child was denied a place at a Church of England school which had as an admission criterion, 'families who attend the Church of England'. The family did attend but were still turned down. The admission authority claimed that what it meant was that families must have attended at least twice monthly for at least five years. That was not stated in the policy.

At another admission authority for a Roman Catholic school, a child was denied a place because although the letter the parents obtained from the priest did say they were practising Catholics, it did not say how often the family attended church. However, there was nothing in the admission criteria requiring such information; the letter merely had to prove that the family was a practising Catholic family.

Maintaining objectivity in such circumstances is difficult if the criterion is not phrased very carefully. There can be no suggestion that parents are in any way competing with each other to see who is the more religious.

> **CASE STUDY**
> Mr A and Mrs B appealed against a decision not to admit their child to a Catholic primary school. The first priority was given to 'baptised children of committed Catholic parents'. Mr A and Mrs B had their child baptised after the closing date for applications but before the admission committee met to consider its decision. However, the governors interpreted the criterion as meaning that the child had to be baptised before the closing date for applications, and therefore denied the child a place. This was ruled to be unjust, as the criterion did not specify when the child had to be baptised.

Things to consider
- Are the faith criteria clear and objective?
- Did you provide the evidence that was required? What exactly *was* required?

Children with special educational needs or disabilities

If your child has a statement of special educational need, and that statement names the school, the school is under a legal duty to admit your child. The governing body, even if it is the admission authority, may not refuse admission. If they do attempt to refuse a place, then you can appeal. Such appeals are held under different legislation, to a different body and under a different code, and are outside the scope of this book. You should speak to the Local Authority that covers the school.

Many authorities rightly give priority to children with special needs, but it should be clear from the admission criteria what evidence is needed to qualify. Children with recognised special educational needs that fall short of a statement must not be treated any differently from other applicants.

Even if the admission authority does not specifically give priority to children with special needs, if your child is on the special needs register it would be worth mentioning it as part of your appeal.

Although the admission authority may not have been able to give any weight to it as part of their decision, the appeal panel can.

LEGAL POINT

Admission authorities may not refuse to admit a pupil because they consider themselves unable to cater for his or her special educational needs. Admission authorities must consider applications from children who have special educational needs but no statement, on the basis of the school's published admission criteria. They cannot refuse to admit a pupil on the grounds that he or she does not have a statement of special educational needs, or is currently being assessed for one.

School Admissions Code of Practice, paragraph 7.19

Children with disabilities should be treated in the same way as any other applicant. Schools have a duty to make reasonable adjustments to ensure that pupils with disabilities are not placed at a substantial disadvantage, although this does not apply to the provision of auxiliary aids and services or to physical adaptations to buildings.

If your child suffers from a disability as defined by the Disability Discrimination Act (a pupil has a disability if he or she has a physical or mental impairment that has a substantial and long-term adverse effect on his or her ability to carry out normal day-to-day activities), then it is essential for you to make this clear in your application to the school.

LEGAL POINT

Since September 2002, Part IV of the Disability Discrimination Act 1995 (inserted by the Special Educational Needs and Disability Act 2001) has applied with regard to access to education. Schools and LEAs must not treat disabled children less favourably than other pupils for a reason relating to their disability, and must make reasonable adjustments to ensure that disabled pupils are not placed at a substantial disadvantage compared with non-disabled children. Schools and admission authorities must not discriminate against a disabled child in the arrangements they make for determining admission to the school; in the terms on which they offer admission; and by refusing or deliberately omitting to accept an application for admission.

School Admission Appeals Code of Practice, paragraph 2.13

Things to consider
- If your child has a statement and has been turned down, you must approach the Local Authority. A school has no right to refuse admission to a child who has a statement which names that school.
- If your child has special needs or disabilities, but not a statement, they must be treated in the same way as every other child.
- If your child has disabilities and is denied a place, then the appeal panel must consider if your child's condition had any part to play in the decision. If it did, then the decision may be unlawful.

Waiting lists

As soon as your child is turned down, contact the admission authority immediately and ask if they run a waiting list. If they do, get on it as soon as you possibly can. Many authorities automatically place children who are appealing onto the list – but don't rely on it.

> *Many admission authorities maintain waiting lists, although they are not obliged to do so. Some admission authorities maintain a waiting list until a month or so after the admission date, to fill places that may become available at the beginning of the school year. As long as being on a waiting list does not raise undue expectations about the likelihood of being offered a place in due course, it can be helpful to parents to know where they stand if places should subsequently become available at the school. Where a waiting list is used, the school's published admission policy should make clear that these children will be ranked in the same order as the published oversub- scription criteria.*
> *School Admissions Code of Practice, paragraph 7.29*

Placing your child's name on the list is not an alternative to appealing, nor does it affect your right of appeal, but you may be lucky and be offered a place without the need to appeal. Waiting-list arrangements should be clear, fair and objective, and must not give priority based simply on the date on which the application was added to the list. However, despite clear guidance that such practices are not allowed, a few admission authorities do still run a waiting list based on chronological order of application. Get your name on the list as soon as possible, just in case your admission authority is running its procedures in that way – even if it shouldn't.

You should ask where you are on the list, but be warned that if new applicants have a higher priority under the oversubscription criteria, they will be ranked higher on the list and you will be bumped down a place. Length of time on the waiting list does not determine your priority.

Where places become vacant before any admission appeals are heard, admission authorities should fill these vacancies from any waiting list. Placing a child's name on a waiting list does not affect the parent's right of appeal against an unsuccessful application and should not be used in any way against you in the appeal.

CHAPTER 2

How to lodge your appeal

How to lodge your appeal. Admissions outside the normal admission round. Timetable of events. On what grounds can I appeal? How to plan your appeal strategy. Dealing with the allocated school. Obtaining references. The appeal is about your child, not about you. Other sources of information. Submitting your appeal

How to lodge your appeal

This is likely to be a very difficult time. Receiving the letter telling you that your child is not going to the school you have set your heart on is a distressing and upsetting experience. Naturally you are likely to be angry, and very worried for your child and for their future. This is not the best time to be thinking too much about the ins and outs of your appeal.

If you applied to a school and were unsuccessful, then you must receive a letter telling you that your child has not been offered a place and giving the reason(s) why. Admission authorities have rightly been criticised for sending letters that failed to state clearly why they turned down an application. The letter must also tell you that you have a right to appeal to an independent appeal panel, and must explain how you do that.

LEGAL POINT
Where a child has been refused entry to a school, parents should receive, in writing, full reasons why the application was unsuccessful, in light of the published admission criteria for the school. The letter to parents must inform them of their right of appeal, including details of how to make an appeal (a pre-printed form can be used) and the person to whom they should send their notice of appeal.
School Admission Appeals Code of Practice, paragraph 4.4

At this stage you need do no more than state your intention to appeal. Some admission authorities send out letters that include lines such as, 'You must state clearly your reason for objecting to the decision, quoting the relevant criterion/criteria of the admission policy.' This is wrong. At this stage you are under no obligation whatsoever to state your reasons for appeal.

Many admission authorities include a pre-printed form that should be a useful guide. Do not feel under any pressure to start making your case. Simply return the form, or write a letter, saying that you wish to appeal against the decision not to admit your child. A sample letter is set out in Appendix 3.

Some admission authorities have been criticised for letters that appeared to suggest grounds under which appeals could be successful, or to state that appeals can only be on technical grounds. The Local Government Ombudsman, who has an oversight responsibility for school appeals, has rightly criticised authorities for such letters.

The letter that you receive may very well include a term such as 'prejudice' – for example, 'To admit your child would cause prejudice to the provision of efficient education and the efficient use of resources.' This is a phrase that during the whole admission process you may well hear and see over and over again: basically, it is a very legalistic way of saying that the school is full. Unfortunately, despite advice from the government not to use the term as it is felt to be too legalistic, it is still used sometimes in letters to parents.

The letter must also give you the closing date by which you must lodge your appeal. The recommended period is not less than 14 days (or ten working days) from the receipt of the letter. It would be unreasonable for this period to be any shorter, and in the unlikely event of an admission authority giving a much reduced timescale, this would be something that an appeal panel would need to consider very carefully. Try to keep to the given deadline. Sometimes parents submit a late appeal because of difficult circumstances or because they did not understand what was required. Admission authorities should not unreasonably refuse to accept a late appeal, and appeal panels are generally sympathetic – but in general, late submissions do not make a very good impression.

At this stage start some very basic administration. Buy a file and keep a copy of everything. Photocopy any forms you return and keep a copy of any letter or email you send. It is also a good idea to send all letters via recorded delivery: this means that you have proof of posting and that the recipient must sign for it. There have been cases lost when paperwork went astray and parents were unable to prove that they had in fact submitted it on time. Mark any letter that you receive with the date on which it arrived; you should also make a note of any telephone conversations you have with the admission authority, and keep details in your file. That may sound bureaucratic, but it can be important if, for example, the Headteacher or anyone else in authority at the school or Local Authority suggests that you should have a place, or in any way led you to believe that you had a place. Such things can have an impact on your appeal.

The letter you receive from the admission authority should include the address to whom you should send your reply. If it doesn't, then send your letter to your Local Authority for Community and Voluntary Controlled schools, and to the school itself for Foundation and Voluntary Aided schools. If you are in any doubt at all, call the school and check. Do try to make sure you send your reply to arrive by the deadline.

Some admission authorities will send acknowledgement of your intention to appeal. Check that your authority will let you know when your papers arrive. If it does not routinely send out acknowledgements, then ask if it will do so for you – or if it will let you include a stamped addressed postcard. Getting a letter confirming that your appeal has been lodged will do a lot to put your mind at rest: you will know that the wheels have started turning.

Things to consider
- Did the letter give you a deadline for applications? If so, make sure you try and stick to it as far as possible.
- You do not have to say *why* you are appealing at this stage – just that you are.
- Did the letter suggest any limitations on your appeal? If so, make a note as this may be relevant later.
- Was it made clear to whom you should send the reply? If not, contact the school.
- Start keeping a file of all your correspondence, emails, notes about phone calls, etc. Keep copies of everything. Send all letters via recorded post. Date every letter when it arrives.

Admissions outside the normal admission round

Most of the information in this book does not differentiate between appeals made during the normal admission round – that is, the period to determine admissions for September – and appeals made at any other time. Some primary schools may have two or three term intakes, admitting children in January and at the start of the Summer term. However, their applications will be considered as if they were to be admitted in September and then held over.

Admissions outside the normal admission round are handled differently, although the same considerations apply. If the year group into which your child will go has space (in other words, if it comprises fewer children than the school's published admission number) then the school must admit your child. If the year group is at the published number, the admission authority may allow your child to be admitted if they feel that this would not cause problems for the school or for the children already attending. However, if they feel that it would cause problems then the authority will turn down your application. The letter of refusal must inform you of your right to an independent appeal panel.

In terms of the actual appeal process itself, there is no difference between appeals in the normal admission round and those outside it.

Timetable of events

The School Admission Appeals Code of Practice – the official guidance for appeal panels – says that appeals should be heard within 'a reasonable time'. The suggested timescale is 30 school days from submitting your appeal, or in the case of the normal admission round, 30 school days from the date by which appeals had to be lodged.

Appeals must not be heard before the deadline has passed.

Given that most offers for places at a school are likely to be made around the beginning of March, and taking into account school holidays, your appeal may therefore not be heard until the end of April/beginning of May. Were an appeal to be held significantly later than the recommended period of 30 school days, an appeal panel may consider whether this acted against the parent. Even if the appeal panel did not consider this, then the Local Government Ombudsman (see Chapter 7) might do so as part of a case for maladministration.

You should receive written notice of the date of your appeal at least 14 days (ten working days) before the hearing. Occasionally panels may offer to hear your appeal sooner – perhaps because another parent has withdrawn their appeal, or because the panel is having trouble timetabling. Many parents are tempted to agree to this shorter notice period, wanting to get it over with, but think carefully. While you may want to put an end to the uncertainty, you don't want to rush things and risk going into the appeal half-prepared.

Some admission authorities helpfully give an indication of the period during which your appeal is likely to be heard – often letting you know not long after the closing date and once all the appeals have been lodged. This can be a great help if you have to make childcare arrangements, take time off work, plan holidays and so on. The more notice you get, the better you can prepare.

At least seven days before the hearing you must receive the admission authority's written case. This should give full and detailed reasons, with supporting evidence, as to why the authority turned down your application. (This will be looked at in more detail in the next chapter.) However, you must start to plan your appeal long before the school's written case arrives. It would be very difficult to plan an appeal in only seven days.

Things to consider
- Will you be available for the appeal dates? Do you need to make arrangements for work, etc.?
- Are you prepared to waive your 14-day notice?

On what grounds can I appeal?

The simple answer is that you can appeal on any grounds you like, not just that you feel the admission process was incorrectly applied. (Your chances of success will vary quite dramatically, however, according to which grounds you choose.) Nor are you limited to basing your appeal on just one factor: you can appeal on as many grounds as you wish.

The appeal panel is required by law to look at three factors in order:

1 Were the admission criteria correctly applied to your application? If not, and if they had been correctly applied, would your child have been offered a place?
2 If the criteria were correctly applied, is the school full?
3 If the school is full then the panel will have to balance up the problems faced by your child if he or she does not go to the school against the problems faced by the school if they take an extra child (this is known as a 'balancing exercise').

If you were applying for your child to join an infant class (up to the age of seven) and were refused a place because of the class-size limit of 30, this is known as 'infant class size prejudice'. In such hearings the panel's options are limited, with the result that these appeals are much harder to win. For more detail, see Chapter 8.

How to plan your appeal strategy

Appeal panels are made up of people, the vast majority of whom are extremely sympathetic to a parent's plight. One appeal-panel member said, 'We will bend over backwards to help a parent and give them a considerable amount of leeway.' It might be an overstatement to say that panels want you to win, but the resounding majority will go out of their way to ensure that you, the parent, are given every opportunity to present your case, and given all the help the panel can offer.

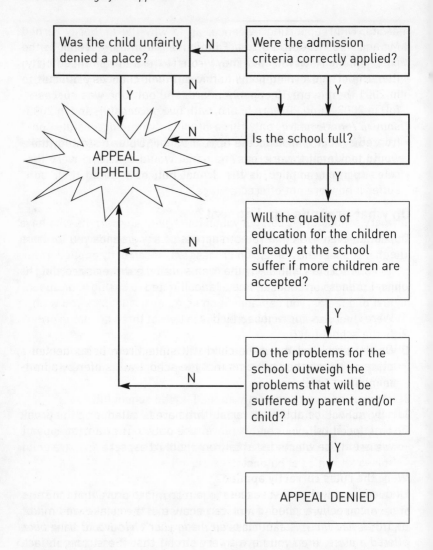

But that being said, winning an appeal is not easy. Nationally, only about one in three appeals is successful, and locally you may find the record much worse than that. The more thoroughly you plan your appeal, the better your chances become. Planning an appeal is not quite as hard as it may sound. The rejection letter you received from the admission authority should have given you a detailed explanation as to why your application was unsuccessful. That gives you the basis on which to begin. Start by asking other parents who went to appeal at the same school. Find out what strategies they used and if they were successful. If so, can you use the same approach? If you are applying for a place at secondary school then ask your current

CASE STUDY

Mr and Mrs R appealed to a Foundation secondary school for a place for their son in 2004. They wrote to the admission authority (the school's governing body) to find out their chances of success. In 2001 there were 18 appeals heard, and only one was successful; in 2002 some 20 were heard, with five successful; and in 2003 some 27 were heard, only three of which were successful. Confronted by such a low success rate, they had to plan a strategy that would tackle all three areas the panel would consider: were the rules correctly applied; is the school full; how would their son suffer if he were not offered a place?

primary school if they can put you in touch with any parents who have appealed, even if they were not successful. You can learn a lot from them.

You should plan a strategy that deals with the three aspects of the appeal process (in order of importance):

1 Were the rules correctly applied?
2 Is the school full?
3 Do the problems that your child will suffer from being denied a place outweigh the problems that the school will suffer by admitting him or her?

Ideally you will be able to cover all three areas, although it may well be that realistically you can only cover one or two. The hardest appeals to win are those which rest solely on the third aspect.

Were the rules correctly applied?

Unquestionably the most successful strategy is to prove that the rules were incorrectly applied. If you can show that a mistake was made, and that *had the mistake not been made your child would have been offered a place*, then you have a very strong case. So strong, in fact, that it could be worth approaching the admission authority directly before the appeal is heard and pointing out the facts of the case. If the authority agrees with you that a mistake was made and that your child has been wrongly denied a place, it may well admit your child without going to appeal. Even if it doesn't, you haven't lost anything, as you would still be going to appeal anyway.

If you can prove that a mistake was made, but are unable to prove that the mistake would have benefited your child, it is still worthwhile using the fact of the error when you write your case for an appeal. It could help you. For example, if you can show a catalogue of mistakes with the way in which the whole admission process was handled, this

> **LEGAL POINT**
> *The panel will also need to consider whether the oversubscription criteria for the school were correctly and impartially applied to the pupil concerned, and if not, whether this led to the child in question being refused admission, whereas proper application of the criteria would have led to their acceptance. In that case, the panel should uphold the appeal.*
> School Admission Appeals Code of Practice, paragraph 4.61

might be enough to persuade the appeal panel that they cannot have confidence in how well the admission authority has done its job. It is an old courtroom trick: if you can discredit a witness sufficiently, then anything they say will lack credibility. 'If you can't get this right, then how can we have any confidence that you have got anything else right?' is what you want the panel to be thinking. It is an aggressive tactic, and one that must be handled carefully – but it can be very effective in undermining the admission authority's case.

Fortunately most admission authorities are very diligent and mistakes are not common. But they do occur. We have looked already at some of the troublesome admission criteria (see Chapter 1). If you are applying to a faith school, pay particular attention to the exact wording of the admission criteria. The admission authority must apply the criteria as they are written, not how they want them to be interpreted. Likewise, as we have already examined, make sure that the distance tie-breaker is accurate. If a child is admitted who has no greater claim to a place than your own child but who lives further away, then you should be well placed for a successful appeal. (But before leaping in, do make sure that they are of an equal priority. They might for example have a sibling at the school, or have a statement which has named the school, or have more than one legitimate address – e.g. have parents who are separated.)

If there is any room for doubt about how the admission process was conducted then it is worth writing this into your appeal – you may have a case. There is nothing to be lost and a lot to be gained. Look very hard indeed at the rules and how they were applied.

Signs that you may not have a case

✗ The admission criteria were correctly applied.
✗ The authority uses a geographical information system database to calculate distances, rather than measuring them.

61

Monday 12.5.01

Colkerron from Rainbow
ISBN 97807 136 82366

Mrs Spears
£9.99 - Cash

Signed

Is the school full?

This is the hardest aspect of an appeal to prepare, as most of the information you need will not be available until the case for the admission authority drops through your letterbox some seven days before the appeal hearing. We will cover how to read and understand the authority's case in some detail in the next chapter, but nevertheless there is some groundwork you can do before their case arrives. If the school is not full then you have a cast-iron case. Admission authorities may not refuse applications to a school if the school has spaces available (unless it is a fully selective grammar school or a state-run boarding school – see Chapter 8).

> *If applications are made for available places, admission authorities should admit pupils up to their school's published admission number as they have a statutory duty to comply with parental preference. They should not hold back or reserve places, e.g. in the expectation that there may be later applications from families moving into the catchment area.*
>
> *School Admissions Code of Practice, paragraph 7.9*

> *Admission authorities may allocate places in advance of the family moving to the area, when they have suitable confirmation, such as proof of exchange of contracts, a letting agreement, or a letter from an employer or Service person's commanding officer, confirming details of relocation. If there are places available, but more applicants than places, the published oversubscription criteria should be applied. Parents applying for places in a full school should be informed of their right of appeal.*
>
> *School Admissions Code of Practice, paragraph 7.31*

Nor are admission authorities permitted to reserve places in the expectation of later arrivals – although they are entitled to offer a place to a family that has yet to move into an area if they have proof that the family will be resident (e.g. contracts for a house purchase have been exchanged).

> **LEGAL POINT**
> *Although they are not allowed to reserve places for blocks of these children [Children of UK Service personnel and other Crown servants (including Diplomats)], admission authorities may accept applications from parents returning to their area some months in advance and may allocate a school place.*
>
> *School Admissions Code of Practice, paragraph 7.28*

Establishing whether a school is full or not is a key part of the appeal. If you can show that the school is not really full although the authority may claim it, then you stand a good chance of winning. But what does it mean for a school to be 'full'?

Every mainstream school in England and Wales should have gone through a process called the net capacity calculation, designed to measure its exact size and the number of children it can accommodate. This extensive survey was designed to standardise and simplify the way in which schools calculate their capacity, using a series of measurements and calculations to allow every school to work out exactly how many pupils it can hold. By dividing the total number of pupils by the number of year groups, it gave an indication of how many children could be accommodated in each year, and therefore how many to admit: this is called the 'indicated admission number'.

CASE STUDY
Mr C and Ms H appealed against a Local Authority primary school that had refused to admit their daughter. The published admission number had been set at 22 for many years, but the school had been redeveloped a year prior to their application. The couple were able to show that the published admission number did not truly reflect the school's capacity. The appeal was upheld.

School admission authorities are required to set their actual admission figure – known as the 'published admission number' (PAN) – generally to be no lower than the indicated admission number. Schools are free to set a PAN that is higher than the indicated number, and many do. Only in certain exceptional circumstances is an admission authority allowed set a PAN lower than the indicated number (this would mean that the school would be accepting fewer children than it had the space for – not a very efficient use of resources).

For the purposes of your appeal the PAN is an important number. An admission authority can only start applying its admission criteria when it has reached its PAN, so if you can show that the PAN is too low then you stand a good chance of persuading the appeal panel to admit your child.

Calculating a school's net capacity is an expensive and time-consuming process and does not need to be done every year. It only needs updating if physical changes are made to the usable space of a school, such as: space being removed or more space being added; several small spaces being converted into one larger one; or changes being made that affect the type of space in classrooms. Often schools will have building work done but not update their published admission number.

Find out when the PAN was set, and what, if any, development there has been since that date. If the school has recently undergone expansion or development, it could be that its net capacity figure has not been updated and this may help your case. If you can show that the school has underestimated its capacity and can take more children than it claims, then you would be in a good position to challenge the admission authority's decision not to admit your child. In the next chapter we will look in more detail at the net capacity figure and how to use it.

LEGAL POINT
It is not enough for the admission authority to show that the admission number has been reached; it should also demonstrate what prejudice would be caused by the additional admission ... The appeal panel should be satisfied that the school's published admission number is a justified limit.
School Admission Appeals Code of Practice, paragraph 4.61

There is another way to 'attack' the question of a school's capacity. The Appeals Code of Practice is very clear on this point: it is not sufficient for an admission authority to say that the admission number has been reached; they must also show what problems admitting your child would cause – or, in the language of the appeal, what prejudice would be caused. This is covered in more detail in Chapter 3, but at this stage there is not much more you can do. Until you see the detail of the admission authority's case, which you will not receive until seven days before the hearing, you will not have all the information about the prejudice they are claiming.

Do the problems that your child will suffer from being denied a place outweigh the problems that the school will suffer by admitting him or her?
This is by far the hardest aspect of the appeal to win. Realistically many parents – probably most – find themselves fighting on this ground. In order to be successful you must show two things: that your child will suffer if he or she does not attend the school; and that the suffering they will endure will be more significant than that which the school will endure if they do. Given that if you do have to fight on this ground, the appeal panel will already have accepted that the admission authority has done its job properly, and that the school is genuinely full and to admit more children to the school will cause it and its existing pupils real and genuine problems, this is a tough – though not impossible – call. In the language of the appeal, this is known as the 'balancing stage'.

The DfES does not keep statistics on why appeals were won and lost, but talking to appeal-panel members, your chances of winning an appeal on these grounds are not as good as your chances if you can show a fault in the admission process. To win at the balancing stage you will need to prove an overwhelming case as to why the particular school you are applying to is the only school that can satisfy your needs. You are not arguing a case *against* your allocated school; you must argue *for* your desired school.

'Prejudice' – how do I know if I have a strong case?

There must be no doubt in the panel's mind that you and/or your child will suffer greatly if he or she is not admitted. This doesn't mean that you and/or your family will be inconvenienced, or put out, or upset: you must be able to show real and genuine problems.

Problems that appeal panels do not generally consider to be overwhelming include:

Travel by public transport

Panels do not tend to look favourably on claims that 11 year olds can't travel by bus/train, etc. on their own. Unless they have some particular need (such as a disability) then it would be hard to win a case based solely on your secondary-school child having to catch a bus. You may have a stronger case if for example the bus journey is very far, or if it would necessitate a long walk to the bus stop, or if there were an unreasonable number of changes.

Appeals to primary schools may have more luck, since sending a primary aged child unaccompanied on public transport could well be considered unreasonable. However, this would depend very much on circumstances, and you would have to prove a case for why this was the only alternative. (Why this school? Couldn't other parents take the child, or someone else accompany them? How difficult would it be to make other arrangements? Will the Local Authority not provide transport?)

CASE STUDY

Mr L and Ms H appealed against a rural VA secondary school that had refused to admit their daughter. They claimed that the bus journey to the school using public transport was too far for a young girl to make by herself. The panel disagreed, saying that a ten-mile journey without a change was not unreasonable for an 11-year-old child to undertake. They pointed out that other children attending the same school would be on the bus with her. The appeal was denied.

Minor medical conditions

It is very common for parents to claim that their child suffers from asthma/eczema/nosebleeds. This may well be true, but is it an overwhelming condition? To stand any chance of success you would need evidence that your child's condition was indeed serious (a letter from a GP or hospital, for example); you would also need to show why the school to which you were appealing was particularly well suited to deal with the problem.

> **CASE STUDY**
> Mr and Mrs P appealed against the refusal to admit their son to a Community secondary school. Their son had a serious medical condition that had several times necessitated emergency treatment in the past. They were keen that he attend a school near to the hospital. The allocated school – the closest to his home – was on the other side of the borough. The school did not give priority to children who could demonstrate a medical need and the boy's condition had not been mentioned on their application. Mr and Mrs P were able to show an exceptional need, supported by a letter from the consultant. The appeal was upheld.

Special educational needs

If your child has a statement, and the school is named on that statement, then the panel may instruct the school to take him or her. Otherwise the statement is not of itself a compelling reason for admission. If you could prove that your child had been discriminated against because of their special need, you might have grounds under disability discrimination legislation (see pp. 73–4). You may have a stronger case if the school to which you are applying has some particular strength in dealing with special needs.

Bullying

A very emotional case on which to fight. Parents of bullied children quite rightly feel very passionate and may find it difficult to accept that they have anything but a cast-iron case. If you can prove bullying (a letter from a Headteacher, for example) then that may be grounds for appealing against a particular school, if the bully is going to that school. However, bullying itself may not be sufficient grounds for why a child should be granted a place at a particular school. You may have more of a case if the school to which you are appealing has a reputation for effective pastoral care and you could show that your child was strongly in need of it.

All his/her friends are going there
Again, unlikely to be a strong enough argument on its own, although it would certainly be worth mentioning as part of a more general appeal. It is quite commonplace for children to go to schools on their own, and an appeal panel could reasonably expect a child to make new friends at a new school. You may have a stronger case if you could link this with some emotional special need. Some panels may look favourably on an appeal based on a claim of belonging to a particular community and your child being denied a place within that community. This can be difficult to reconcile with charges of racism. A panel cannot lawfully discriminate on the basis of race, so, for example, you would be unlikely to win an appeal on the basis that your child would be in a minority ethnic group at a school.

Family circumstances
Almost impossible to generalise, but if you can show that the school to which you are appealing is the only one that will not cause your family severe problems – in getting them to school, for example – then a panel may look kindly on your application. You have a stronger case if you can produce convincing evidence to support your claim.

Personal/religious belief
This can be quite a strong case if you have the evidence to back it up, or can produce a good argument. Cases have been won over a strongly held view for single-sex education, but these were exceptional circumstances. If you genuinely hold very strong beliefs about education, and can show that the particular school to which you are applying is the only school that matches those beliefs, then that would be a strong factor to put in your case.

Your child's particular strengths
If you can show that your child has a particular strength in a subject, and the school to which you are applying matches that strength, then that is a factor that appeal panels have looked favourably on in some cases. Again, you would need to produce strong evidence of your child's record, and to prove that this wasn't just a negotiating tactic.

Dealing with the allocated school

In order to win your appeal at the balancing stage, you must show an overwhelming case for your child to attend that particular school. And to do that, you may have to argue against the school to which your child has been given a place (if he or she has been awarded one). This can be difficult. If you are appealing for a place at a Local

Authority school (Community or VC) you may well simultaneously be arguing for a place at one school and against a place at another.

Appeal panels do not look favourably on parents who simply 'run down' other schools; you will need good reasons to show why a school is the wrong one for your child. First you must find out as much as you can about the school that has offered your child a place. Talk to local parents by all means, but you must make your own decisions. It is essential to visit the school and form your own opinions.

You can also download the school's latest Ofsted report from the Ofsted website (www.ofsted.gov.uk). Take care with these: reports can be up to five years old and may be based on old information. The older the report, the less reliable it is. When you have downloaded the report, scour it. You are looking for information that will back up your case. So if you are saying that your child has been bullied previously, for example, look for anything in the report that suggests bullying or general discipline problems at the school. If you are saying that your child is very academic, look for evidence that the allocated school will not suit them (poor results, a negative atmosphere, etc.). Do the same if he or she is particularly sporty, or has other strengths that the chosen school cannot match, but the school to which you are appealing can.

Make plenty of notes about the school, as you will need the information when you come to write your appeal.

Obtaining references

It will help your case considerably if you can back it up with some kind of reference from a third party who can support your appeal – and in some cases a reference is essential. For example, if you are claiming a medical condition, then at the very least you should have supporting references from your GP. A letter from a specialist would be much more impressive. It would be exceptionally hard to win an appeal based on medical grounds without sound supporting evidence.

Likewise if you claim that family hardship is a problem, then try to obtain evidence – a letter from social services, for example. If you claim that work problems would mean you giving up your present job, then get a letter from your employer. If you claim transport problems then get a copy of the timetable to help your case.

It is always worth obtaining additional references that will help the appeal panel to form a more complete impression of your child. You should at the very least get a letter of support from your child's Headteacher, and you may want to consider other people who might support your application: perhaps a minister, even if you are not applying to a church school, or a sports coach – anyone in fact who can write about your child and will paint a favourable impression of them. Although this is not strictly relevant to the appeal, your aim is to win a place for your child. If you can help the panel understand more about him or her as a person, it may well help you. It may be that the panel completely ignores character references, in which case you have lost nothing; but panels are obliged at the least to read all the evidence put to them.

The appeal is about your child, not about you

Some parents make the profound mistake of thinking that the appeal is in some way about them; that somehow they are being judged by the school, so that if they are in some way 'better' parents then this will positively affect their chances of success.

It may come as a hard blow, but the panel doesn't care that you have been a school governor at your child's school for four years, or that you have been a stalwart member of the PTA or Friends association and have raised thousands of pounds. Nor indeed that you listen to children read every week, teach them football, go on school trips or any other activity. None of it is relevant to the case in hand. Don't mention it. It is not relevant.

Equally, if you don't do any of those things, either because you don't want to or because you can't, it makes not one jot of difference to the likelihood of success of your case.

Nor is the panel going to judge your appeal on how well you can write or spell, how you talk, your accent, your clothes, your background, your colour, your religion, your address, your appearance, or any of the thousands of other things that parents often worry about.

That is not to say that you should not take care, dress well on the day, and make sure that your appeal is as well presented as you can ... but at the hearing itself it is what you have to say that matters, and nothing else.

Other sources of information

You should definitely get hold of a copy of the official government documentation on admissions. There are two free guides, which are quoted at length throughout this book. These are *The School Admissions Code of Practice*, and *The School Admission Appeals Code of Practice*. Both of them are statutory documents which admission authorities must follow; unfortunately neither is written for parents (they are written for admission authorities and/or members of appeal panels), nor are they particularly easy to understand. Nevertheless they are very important documents and will give you a background in the legal points of the whole process.

To obtain copies, contact: DfES Publications, PO Box 5050, Sherwood Park, Annesley, Nottingham NG15 0DJ. Tel: 0845 6022260 Fax: 0845 6033360 Textphone: 0845 6055560 email: dfes@prolog.uk.com

To order *The School Admission Appeals Code of Practice*, quote the following reference: DfES/0030/2003. To order *The School Admissions Code of Practice*, quote DfES/0031/2003.

Submitting your appeal

You are now in a position to draft your appeal and submit it. If you have been given any instructions about when you should submit your written appeal, you need to pay heed to them. Some admission authorities may ask for your case as much as a month in advance of the hearing; others may be more generous. You will not be penalised for submitting your case late, but it will be helpful to you to submit it within the timescale.

> **LEGAL POINT**
> *Parents should also be informed that there is no statutory time limit for submitting information about their appeal, and that they may be able to submit information after lodging their appeal, but before the hearing.*
> **School Admission Appeals Code of Practice, paragraph 4.30**

With luck you will have an appeal that addresses the three areas the panel will consider: were the rules followed properly; is the school really full; do my child's needs outweigh those of the school? Realistically, parents who can appeal on all three grounds are not common. If your appeal cannot cover all three grounds, then start with the strongest case.

Structure your appeal to look at all three if you can. Begin with the most important: 'I do not believe that the admission procedures at Blanktown School were correctly applied because...' Then list, in as much detail as you can, exactly the reasons for this. Think out your case and then write it in as logical a way as you can. It helps if you can talk it through with a friend or colleague. If you can convince them, with luck your case may hold water.

The next part of your appeal should address the issue of whether the school is really full – covered in some detail in the next chapter. It may well be that you are not able to fully comment on this issue until you get the detailed information from the admission authority, and that may not be until seven days before your hearing. However, if you have any evidence relevant to this area to support your argument, put it down now.

The next part of your appeal should address the needs of your child, and should help the panel weigh up your child's needs and those of the school. Describe your child to the panel. What is he or she good at? What are his or her strengths and weaknesses? Does he or she have any special needs, or a disability? Has he or she been bullied at school? Does he or she suffer from anxiety? Are there social problems? Be sure to describe your child's strengths, too. What is his or her performance like at school? What is he or she expected to achieve? Does he or she like sport? Is he or she academic? Is he or she very sociable? Remember that you are trying to shift the balance in your child's favour; to prove that they will suffer if they do not attend the school.

Then explain in as much detail as possible why this school is the right one for your child. Is it very academic/sporty? Does it have strong pastoral support/good special educational needs provision? What about your child's peer group? Are most of his or her friends going there? Although these things on their own may not be sufficient to win your appeal, it will stand you in good stead if you can prove an overall picture of problems if your child is not admitted.

The next stage is one that you need to handle especially carefully – showing why your allocated school (if you have one) is not the right place for your child. Do not launch into an emotional attack on the school; do not report rumour as fact; do not spread gossip. Stick to the facts. Try to use the Ofsted report to back up anything you say about the school. If the Ofsted report doesn't back it up, then write something along the lines of 'when I visited the school, I felt that ...' and recount your experience. Leave the panel in no doubt that you have done your research, that you have visited the school, spoken to people, read the reports. They will not look favourably on cases that simply say things like 'everyone knows that Loamshire High is a sink school with a terrible reputation'.

When you have written your appeal, check it very carefully. Are there spelling mistakes? Is it completely clear what you mean? Have you got the evidence to back up your statements? Get a friend – or better, more than one – to check it for you. Ask them to read it through. Does it make sense? Do they understand it? If your friend or colleague doesn't understand it, then change it.

When you are quite happy with the final document, photocopy everything and send your statement and the original copies of all your references to the address given, using recorded delivery.

CHAPTER 3

The case for the admission authority

When will I receive information from the admission authority? The admission authority's case. Prejudice to the provision of efficient education and the efficient use of resources. What information you need, and where to find it. How does a school know how many pupils to admit? Common spaces (halls and dining areas, corridors, stairs, toilets, etc.). Other factors to consider. Pupil:teacher ratios. Advice given to appellants

When will I receive information from the admission authority?

The admission authority should acknowledge receipt of your appeal, and helpful authorities should give you some indication, if they know, of the provisional dates of the appeal hearing.

It is not uncommon for many authorities to send you a letter some time after you have lodged your appeal, asking you to confirm your intention to go ahead with the appeal. Do not be surprised by this: it is simply a way of sorting out those who are serious about appealing. Do ensure that you reply in good time.

Until you get the date of your appeal, you may feel as if you are in a 'phoney war'. Up until now the appeal has seemed some way off; something to worry about, yes – but not right now. But once you have a date, you can bring all the weeks of worry to a focus. Many parents describe this as 'the beginning of the end'.

The letter you receive should give you a date and a venue for the appeal hearing. Unless you have previously agreed to it, your appeal should not be held any sooner than 14 days from receipt of the letter. If it is, or if you cannot make the date and time you have been given, contact the admission authority immediately. Appeal panels will do their best to fit you in when it is convenient, but if your appeal is being heard as part of the normal admission round then it may be one of dozens and such flexibility may simply not be possible.

It cannot be stressed enough that *you must attend the appeal*. Relying on your written case alone, and not taking the opportunities presented by the appeal hearing, will very seriously reduce your chances of success. If you do not attend, for whatever reason, the independent appeal panel will make its decision on the basis of the information in front of it on the day. It is up to you to make sure that you present your case as fully as you think necessary – the panel may well not adjourn to a later date if you do not attend.

Check that you know where the appeal is to be held. How will you get there? Do you know the route? How long will it take? If at all possible make the journey to the venue in advance so you know where you are going and how long it will take you. The last thing you want is to get lost on the day, or to arrive late. Do note that the Code of Practice recommends (but does not insist) that the hearing should not take place at the school that is the subject of the appeal.

If you have special requirements, such as wheelchair access, then is the venue suitable? If English is not your first language you can ask for a translator; you can also request a signer. However, do ensure that you give the panel plenty of notice.

Things to consider

- Have you been given 14 days' notice of the appeal?
- Do you know where the appeal is to be held, and how to get there?
- Did you receive the written case at least seven days before the appeal?
- Do you require special facilities such as disabled access, a signer or a translator?

The admission authority's case

The next thing you will receive – and it must arrive no later than seven days before the hearing – will be the admission authority's case.

This will be the first time you will know the full extent of the case against your application. Although admission authorities are under quite tight legal obligations as to what their case should contain, not all of them follow the regulations. If you feel that the case is insufficient then make a note of its shortfalls; the Local Government Ombudsman has seriously criticised authorities that failed to present sufficient evidence.

The Code of Practice lists the evidence that the admission authority is required to submit.

PREPARATION AND PRODUCTION OF EVIDENCE

At least seven days (five working days) before the hearing (unless parents have waived their right under this guidance to a period of 14 days' notice of their appeal), the admission authority should supply the clerk of the appeal panel with the following documents which should be circulated to the panel members and sent to the parent(s):

- *a written statement summarising how the admission arrangements for the school(s) apply to the parent's application, with any relevant background information. Where the parent's appeal relates to the LEA's administration of coordinated arrangements (e.g. because an error has allegedly been made, or because application of those arrangements has led to the child being offered a place at one of two or more preferred schools they could have been offered), details of coordinated arrangements or a statement from the LEA should be provided;*
- *a written statement summarising the reasons for the decision – for instance, full supporting information that prejudice to the provision of efficient education or use of resources would arise from the admission of the child (or children) concerned. A statement referring to accommodation, class sizes, capacity, etc. should be supported by factual information ... (if considered necessary, evidence can be produced in the form of photographs or a video, as well as layout plans of a building);*
- *where another place has been offered, as identified under coordinated arrangements, either the relevant extract of the published scheme or a statement from the LEA should be provided;*
- *copies of any information or documents which are to be put to the panel at the hearing, including anything which has been submitted by the parents.*

School Admission Appeals Code of Practice, paragraph 4.28

The admission authority is under a lot of direction to be very specific about exactly why your child was refused a place. It is not considered sufficient for an authority simply to say that the school is full and so your child could not be admitted. It is unfortunate that despite such clear instruction from the government, many admission authorities still fail to provide enough information.

If the statement you receive does not answer your questions, the Code of Practice is quite clear about your rights. You can ask for any additional, reasonable information. The Local Government Ombudsman has been highly critical of admission authorities which produce cases that are too brief or lack detail; in some cases, no statement is provided at all until the day of the appeal.

LEGAL POINT
The admission authority must provide all the information reasonably asked of it by the parents so that they are in a position to question the admission authority's case.
School Admission Appeals Code of Practice, paragraph 4.30

In the special report on admission appeals, the Ombudsman said:

'The content of the authority's statement must be adequate. The Appeals Code gives good guidance on this point. We would like to highlight some points and add some supplementary points as follows:

- the document must explain, with full supporting information, why the admission authority considers that the admission of an additional child or children would cause prejudice to efficient education or the efficient use of resources;
- the document must demonstrate the nature of the prejudice (that is, specify what harm would be caused by additional admissions);
- information should include how the year group will be organised and the size of classes (because, for example, there would be a significant difference in how a parent would need to approach the appeal, depending on whether an intake, say, of 240 children would be organised in eight classes of 30 or nine classes of 26/27);
- if classes are small, some reference should be made to the reason for that (for example, that the classrooms are small);
- in respect of the school appealed for, there should be a statement of the breakdown of successful admissions; that is, how many were admitted under each criterion;
- the document for each individual parent should explain why the child was refused a place, with relevant supporting information (for example, if distance from home to school was the explanation, there should be information about what that distance is and what was the furthest distance from home to school for children accepted under the distance criterion);
- there should be sufficient information to enable the panel to reach a proper view on whether the admission criteria were correctly applied, and for parents to be able to prepare any questions and points they want to put;
- if selection by ability was relevant, either for the whole intake or under partial selection arrangements, the document should give information on the test scores for the individual child and the cut-off point for admission under the ability assessment;

- similarly, if there was partial selection by aptitude, there should be a statement with all relevant information explaining why the child was not admitted under that criterion; and
- if the authority claims that infant class size prejudice is involved, that should be stated together with the authority's reason for making that claim, and an explanation of the qualifying measures which would need to be taken and when they would be required.'

Special Report: School Admissions and Appeals

This is a very useful checklist against which to measure the admission authority's case. If it is found wanting in any way, then make notes of the relevant area(s). When we look at the questioning of the admission authority in the hearing itself, it may be a useful appeal tactic.

In the same way that your written appeal should address the main areas of the panel's work, the admission authority's statement should address two issues. It should show how the rules were applied in your case, and why your child was denied a place; and it must show how admitting your child would cause 'prejudice to the provision of efficient education and the efficient use of resources'.

Prejudice to the provision of efficient education and the efficient use of resources

This is the cornerstone of the admission authority's case and you need to try and dislodge it – or at the very least to make it wobble. They will be attempting to prove to the panel that admitting your child – or in the case of multiple appeals, your child and others – will harm the education of the pupils already at the school; either because results will suffer, or because the school is already bursting at the seams and physically can't fit any more children in.

Let's take the two parts separately and deal with them one by one. In many cases it is easier for the admission authority to prove the problems with resources, rather than the more difficult case of proving prejudice of efficient education. Very often written submissions will ignore the latter altogether and concentrate almost entirely on the strain on resources. Alternatively they may attempt to claim prejudice simply by asserting that results suffer with larger class sizes. But do they have the evidence?

Prejudice to the provision of efficient education

What does this actually mean? The key word to note is 'efficient'. A secondary school that had class sizes of, say, ten would not be providing efficient education. It may well produce outstanding results (one would hope so), but it would be tricky for them to argue that that was providing efficient education. (Equally, a school that was producing terrible results would also have its work cut out to prove efficient education – but there again, it is pretty unlikely that anyone would be appealing to send their child to a school like that.)

CASE STUDY

Mr and Mrs A appealed against the decision not to admit their child to a successful, oversubscribed Foundation school. The school claimed prejudice in their submission, although did not provide any evidence in their written case, which concentrated solely on the issue of resources.

The school had excellent results, which they did much to publicise.

Mr and Mrs A obtained the school prospectus that gave details of the number of children in each year group. They were able to show to the panel that the school was producing very good results despite having more children in each year group than the published admission number. Even though the school was 'over full', the results had continued to improve. They were able to use this information, and quote the school's own publicity, to show how well the school did, even though on average each year group had 11 pupils more than it should.

For the school to claim that admitting one child over the admission number would prejudice the provision of efficient education was untenable, since the school was already producing excellent results with 11 extra pupils. The panel allowed ten more children over the published admission number.

Efficient education means providing a good standard of education for the pupils at the school in a 'reasonable' manner. Nowhere is the word reasonable defined, so there is room for the panel to interpret. The trick to undermining the admission authority's case for prejudice of efficient education is to show that the school can still produce very good results even if it is carrying extra pupils.

Prejudice to the efficient provision of resources

For many admission authorities of heavily oversubscribed schools, this is one of the big guns of their argument, and in many cases there is not that much you can do to defend against it. Fortunately the appeal panel is under an obligation to test the admission authority's claims and must be satisfied that the admission number is justifiable.

Typically the admission authority will claim that the school is too small by citing small classrooms; crowded corridors and stairs;

pressure on dining space, playground and sports facilities; the lack of a suitable hall; pressure on classroom usage; Health and Safety issues; or lack of specialist areas (e.g. laboratories, workshops, studios, language labs, etc.). They may also claim that there are insufficient teachers or support staff. We will look at that claim later.

The quality of evidence provided ranges greatly, from simple assertions ('our classrooms are too small') to detailed information about the school and the capacity of the classrooms and other spaces. With changes to how schools define and calculate their capacity, there should be no reason why admission authorities don't provide detailed information.

What information you need, and where to find it

There are two pieces of information you need to build your case to disprove prejudice: how well is the school doing, and how many children are there.

Finding school results is not difficult. By law, the school is required to publish its figures every year, so a simple phone call should be enough. Remember, the admission authority is under an obligation to provide you with any information you may reasonably ask for.

Depending on the age of your child and what sort of school you are appealing to (infant, junior, primary, middle, secondary, upper), you will need to identify what information you should be asking for.

Type of school	Age range	Key stages	What information will I need?	Where can I find the information I need?
Infant	5–7	Key Stage 1	KS1 SATs results (test and teacher assessments). Percentage of children achieving Level 2 or better in English and Maths	Only from the admission authority. KS1 tests are not on the DfES website
Junior	8–11	Key Stage 2	KS2 SATs results (test and teacher assessments). Percentage of children achieving Level 4 or better in English, Maths and Science. From 2004 on, also percentage achieving Level 5	DfES website will have Level 4 results. School will be able to provide fuller information

Type of school	Age range	Key stages	What information will I need?	Where can I find the information I need?
Primary	5–11	Key Stage 1 Key Stage 2	KS1 and KS2 results as above	See above
Middle	8–13	Key Stage 2 Key Stage 3	KS2 SATs results (test and teacher assessments). Percentage of children achieving Level 4 or better in English, Maths and Science. From 2004 on, also percentage achieving Level 5. Key Stage 3: Percentage of children achieving Level 5 or better in English, Maths and Science	Admission authority. DfES website. *Note* KS3 results are not fully reported on the DfES website, but the school will have complete results
Secondary	11–16	Key Stage 3 Key Stage 4	Key Stage 3: Percentage of children achieving Level 5 or better in English, Maths and Science. Key Stage 4: Percentage of pupils achieving 5 or more A*–C At GCSE; percentage of pupils achieving 5 or more GCSE/GNVQ 5+ A*–G	Admission authority. DfES website. *Note* KS3 results are not fully reported on the DfES website, but the school will have complete results
Upper	14–16	Key Stage 4	Key Stage 4: Percentage of pupils achieving 5 or more A*–C at GCSE/GNVQ; percentage of pupils achieving 5 or more GCSE/GNVQ 5+ A*–G	School; DfES website

You also need to know the number of children in the school. This information can be harder to find. The DfES website

(http://www.dfes.gov.uk/performancetables/index_archived.shtml)

will tell you for some phases of school, but not for all: again, you can ask the admission authority for the information.

What you are looking for is evidence that although the year groups may be oversubscribed, the school is still producing good results (see below).

You should also read the latest Ofsted report (available from the admission authority, or you can download it from http://www. Ofsted.gov.uk/). Look for any comments by the inspectors on their concerns: if nothing is mentioned, then that will help your case – if there were serious concerns about overcrowding, Ofsted would certainly mention it. However, be careful in using older reports. Reports can be four or five years old, and a lot can change in a school over that length of time.

How this helps you

You need to show that even if the school has an overcrowding problem, it still produces good results. How have the school's results changed over time? And how has the school roll changed over the same period? Is there a link between the two? If the results show an upward trend, despite the roll getting larger, that is a pretty good indication that the education of the pupils at the school is not being prejudiced.

Experienced computer users may be able to plot the results on a line graph, superimposing the school roll by year on a graph of the results by year. If the results-line were broadly to follow the school roll, then that would be a very useful piece of information showing that despite the increasing number of children at the school, its results continued to go up. That would make it harder for the school to prove its case that increasing numbers were adversely affecting its performance.

Signs that you may not have a case
✗ When you have done the research you find that the improvement in results has started to slow down, plateaued or even begun to fall. In such cases it may well be that there is prejudice.

How does a school know how many pupils to admit?

The process by which a school calculates its capacity is complex and detailed, and is a jumble of statutory and advisory limits (for example, the size of halls is advisory; the ratio of toilets to pupils is statutory). And there is a raft of guidelines and statutes covering everything from playing fields to school kitchens, the detail of which lies beyond the scope of this book. However, there are some simple rules of thumb that will help.

> **CASE STUDY**
> Ms S appealed against a decision not to admit her daughter to a junior school. The Local Authority claimed that the school was full and there was no room for her. The evidence provided in the appeal did show that the classbase was too small for the number of children: however, by questioning, Ms S established that even if the school admitted her child, the class would have the same number of children in it as it had the previous year. As the school had not reported serious problems with the performance of that year, the admission authority was unable to show that admitting her daughter would cause prejudice to the efficient use of resources. The appeal found in favour of Ms S.

Every school in England has to complete a detailed and complete assessment of its buildings and rooms, measuring them, logging what usage they are put to, and calculating their capacity. By applying various weighting factors to the result, the school can calculate how many pupils it can accommodate. This is known as the net capacity.

For primary schools, the net capacity is calculated on the basis of the number and size of spaces designated as 'classbases'. For secondary schools, it is based on the number, size and type of teaching spaces and the age range of the pupils. In both cases, this is checked against the total usable space available, which must be measured, and ensures that there is neither too much nor too little space available to support the core teaching activities.

All the information is recorded on a single form. Some admission authorities will use the form as part of their submission; others will extract the relevant information from it. Many don't provide any information at all. If the information is not included in their case and you feel it would help you, then you are entitled to ask for it (*The School Admission Appeals Code of Practice*, paragraph 4.3).

For the admission authority to prove prejudice it must show that the school is full and that harm is resulting because of this. So when is a school full?

Classrooms
The DfES guidance on classroom size varies depending on what use the room is put to. A classroom of 50m² and a gym of 260m² can both accommodate a class of 30.

Primary

In primary schools (which include infant and junior schools and middle schools deemed primary), most class teaching takes place in a single room (although there may be a few specialist areas such as ICT suites, a library, design and technology rooms, etc.). This classroom is known as a classbase. The minimum area for a classbase for 30 pupils is $49m^2$, but this must be supported by at least a further $14m^2$ of ancillary area, not including the hall. Part of this further area could be in non-teaching spaces such as stores, but it will predominantly be for teaching – either within the overall area of the classroom, or in shared teaching areas.

Secondary

Because of the much wider range of subjects taught at secondary school and the need for more specialist equipment, determining capacity in a secondary school is a much more complicated affair. In secondary schools, classrooms are divided into categories: general teaching classrooms, practical areas, and performance spaces.

- *General teaching classrooms:* Almost half the subjects taught in secondary schools are 'general teaching', normally requiring standard classrooms. These include English, mathematics, modern foreign languages, history, geography, religious education, general studies, and personal, health and social education (citizenship). The smallest general classroom for 30 pupils is $49m^2$. There should be at least three general teaching classrooms for every 150 pupil places.
- *Practical areas:* Practical-based subjects including science, design and technology, art and some vocational courses require a range of specialist teaching spaces. These fall into two types: '*light practical*' such as science laboratories, art rooms, etc. with water, drainage and perhaps gas services and resistant finishes; '*heavy practical*' with fixed machines such as lathes or cookers. Building guidance says there should be at least one science laboratory for every 150 pupils and at least two design and technology spaces or art rooms.
- *Performance spaces:* Music, drama and media studies require spaces with appropriate acoustic properties, and blackout facilities where necessary, with access to a hall for performances to audiences larger than the class group. There should be at least one music, drama or media space.

For a detailed breakdown of the recommended sizes of all the different sorts of secondary classrooms, please see Appendix 2.

How this helps you

If, for example, a class of 25 in a primary school is being taught in a classbase of 60m², it is hard for the admission authority to claim prejudice. And just because a class of 30 is being taught in a classroom smaller than 49m², that doesn't necessarily mean that the admission authority has a case for prejudice. If the school has always had small rooms but is still successful (most older schools, especially those from Victorian times, will have classbases a lot smaller than 49m²) then the admission authority will have to show exactly what prejudice is being caused.

Signs that you may not have a case

✘ Classrooms are substantially below the recommended sizes.

✘ There are comments in the Ofsted reports highlighting inspectors' concerns over accommodation.

✘ The school is already using unsuitable accommodation for teaching (e.g. teaching specialist subjects in general classrooms).

Common spaces (halls and dining areas, corridors, stairs, toilets, etc.)

Admission authorities will frequently cite pressure on common areas, claiming that they were not designed to cater with the number of pupils.

Corridors are calculated in the school's net capacity figure, so the school should be able to provide the exact size of their corridors and a weighting figure that makes allowance for their usage. Again, the admission authority will need to show that it is at capacity and demonstrate the problems that this causes.

Provision of toilets is covered by law, which says there must be one toilet per 20 pupils (600mm of urinal counts as one toilet), rounded up. This is a legal minimum. If the school is below that figure then it has a justifiable case.

It is not uncommon for admission authorities to claim that the school is unable to feed all the children in their dining areas at any one time. The guidelines make provision for this and allow for several sittings (up to three). There is also a difference in the sort of meals provided; 'snack' type cafeteria meals require less space and the official guidelines say that a meal will be consumed in 15 minutes. The more traditional school dinning room with a hot meal requires more space and guidelines allow for 20-minute servings.

At secondary level in new schools with more than 450 pupils, the total area for a hall should include a main hall sufficient for assemblies of at least half the school at one time, examinations, public performances, parents' evenings and community events. At primary level the requirements are less stringent. Although modern schools do require a school hall, it is not possible for a school to claim prejudice simply because it doesn't have a hall.

How this helps you
The claim that shared or common spaces are overstretched is a very common one used by admission authorities. However, there are times when admission authorities will make assertions without the evidence to support it. Asking them to prove that the common areas are overstretched may cause problems for the presenting officer if he or she does not have the net capacity calculations to hand – in which case this helps you to show that the case for prejudice has not been proved.

Signs that you may not have a case
✗ Any evidence from other bodies that there are Health and Safety concerns about overcrowding.
✗ Comments in the Ofsted report about overcrowding.
✗ Heavily overused common areas.
✗ Lack of toilets.

Other factors to consider

Pupil:teacher ratios
Often admission authorities will claim pressure on the curriculum, typically citing the lack of teachers. Although it is relatively easy to see if the school is understaffed, this will only give a general figure: it is possible for a school to be generously staffed across the whole school, but to suffer from acute shortages in certain subjects.

However, the pupil:teacher ratio is a good indicator, and it is relatively easy to calculate. A very rough guide can be obtained by getting a staff list, adding up the number of teachers and dividing it into the number of pupils. Bear in mind, though, that this is not a true figure because not every teacher works full time. You will need to find out from the school which teachers are full time and which part time, and for the latter, what their part-time status is. This is known as their 'full time equivalent' (FTE). A teacher who works three full days a week would be a 0.6FTE; one who worked only half a day a week would be a 0.1FTE. A true pupil:teacher ratio is the ratio of FTE teachers:pupils.

In maintained primary schools in 2006, the pupil:teacher ratio was 22.0:1. In secondary schools it was 16.6:1.

There is a second measure that schools also use, which takes into account all of the staff at the school. This is known as the pupil:adult ratio. It is calculated in exactly the same way but counts all members of staff including non-teaching staff.

In maintained primary schools in 2006, the pupil:adult ratio was 12.8:1. In secondary schools it was 11.7:1.

The national figures are available on the Department for Education and Skills Research and Statistics website (http://www.dfes.gov.uk/rsgateway/index.shtml).

How this helps you

A school may claim to be under-resourced but actually have a very satisfactory pupil:teacher ratio. It may be difficult for a school to claim prejudice if it can be shown that they are significantly better off in staffing than the national average.

Signs that you may not have a case

✗ Very high pupil:teacher ratio. Be careful of simply doing a head count without establishing how many teachers work part time. Job-share and part-time teaching are increasingly popular; in addition, many schools subscribe to 'peripatetic' teachers (that is, teachers who teach at more than one school) in specialist areas such as music.

Advice given to appellants

Included in the case you will receive from the admission authority should be some advice from the admission authority on how the appeal will be conducted. Typically, this advice is fairly brief to the point of terseness – but do read it. If you do not receive any written advice, you should make a note of this: it may be important in the event that your appeal is unsuccessful. You may wish to consider what steps you take after that, including an appeal to the Local Government Ombudsman on the grounds of maladministration (see Chapter 7).

Some authorities have been criticised for sending out misleading information. Such information includes:

- Any statement that comments on your likelihood of success. It would be wrong for the admission authority to pass judgement on this ahead of the hearing, even in the case of infant class size prejudice appeals (see Chapter 8). However, the advice may comment on the limited grounds on which infant appeals can be won.
- Any statement that says you must stipulate which of the admission criteria you are appealing against. Unfortunately it is not uncommon to be told that you must base your appeal on the admission

criteria. This is wholly wrong, and the Local Government Ombuds-man has rightly criticised admission authorities that issue such advice. As we have seen, you may base your appeal on any grounds you choose. It is not up to the admission authority to pre-determine your appeal.

If you feel that the advice you have been given is misleading in any way, then make a note of it. It may help your case.

CHAPTER 4

The appeal hearing

Should you attend the appeal hearing, and what happens if you don't? The panel. What powers does the appeal panel have? Who sits on the panel? The clerk to the appeal. Should you take anyone with you? On the day of the hearing. Who will be there? The order of the hearing. Submission of late documents. How is the appeal run?

So this is it. A period of weeks, and maybe months, of waiting is drawing to a close. By now you will have received notice of the date and venue of your hearing; you will have been sent the admission authority's case; and you should have submitted your own case. But who will 'sit in judgement'? Who gets to decide if your son or daughter is going to be admitted to the school of your choice?

Should you attend the appeal hearing, and what happens if you don't?

Yes. You really should attend. This is your one chance to win that place for your child. If you don't attend, then two things will happen: first, your case will be based entirely on the written evidence you have provided, and there will be no chance for the panel to cross-question you on it. That may sound on the face of it rather a good thing, but it isn't. The panel is there to help you. The members will ask questions not with the intention of 'catching you out', but of eliciting more information to enable them to reach their decision. The second thing that will happen is that the admission authority's case will go unchallenged. Again the panel will be able to ask questions of it, but you won't.

You really must attend the appeal hearing.

The panel

The Independent Admissions Appeal Panel (the panel) is made up of three or five members. It is rare to find panels of five; almost without exception a panel will comprise three members. The rules about who can sit on the panel and who cannot are pretty tight. But before looking at these rules, let us dispel some myths:

The panel is a rubber stamp by 'education insiders'. Far from it. The vast majority of panels are truly independent of the Local Authority or school: indeed, governors and officials often complain about the 'odd' decisions made by panels, saying that they are too lenient, or not rigorous enough. At the same time, appellants also complain about how tough and unsympathetic they are. If both sides complain, then they must be doing something right.

> **CASE STUDY**
> The Local Government Ombudsman reported a case where one member of the panel was a governor at another local school. When the appellant made comments about the school, the panel member said he wished to defend the school and went into some length about why it would suit the child in question. The Ombudsman considered this to be grounds for maladministration.

The panel is only there to decide if the rules were followed correctly. No. The panel will make a ruling on that, but it has complete freedom (except in infant class size prejudice hearings – see pp. 106–12) to consider much more than that. It will listen to anything you say as long as this is relevant and has bearing on the case.

The decision has already been made. It is true that the panel will already have read the written evidence provided, and may have formed early opinions – but it will not make a decision until the hearing is over.

Members are all part of the 'government gravy train'. They may well be, but not by serving on an appeal panel. Members of the panel are not paid to serve. They may claim expenses and a small loss-of-earnings payment, but nothing more.

Much is done to preserve the independence of the panel:

- Parents and education representatives are not present when the panel makes its decisions.
- The panel does not report to, nor is it responsible to, the admission authority, be that a school governing body or a Local Authority.
- The panel has to work within the national statutory School Admission Appeals Code of Practice.

- Members do not sit on panels where they have a conflict of interest.
- The work of the panel is monitored by the Council on Tribunals.
- The decision of the panel is binding on both the Local Authority and the parents.
- The panel's decision cannot be overturned except by court ruling. The Secretary of State has some limited powers, but cannot overrule an appeal.

Until the new Code of Practice came out in 2003, it was quite common for the appeal panel to be given a tour of the school so that the Headteacher or a governor could point out to the panel the conditions at the school. The new Code has rightly stopped this. Although many panel members liked the tours, feeling it gave them a better understanding of the problems of the school, this practice was felt to be against the interests of the parents. If such a tour were to be conducted, it could only be done with all parties present.

LEGAL POINT
Panel members cannot be led on 'tours' of schools to make their own assessments – this would call into question their independence, and could lead to allegations of lobbying.
            School Admission Appeals Code of Practice, paragraph 4.28

What powers does the appeal panel have?

The appeal panel can either refuse or allow your appeal. And that is the limit of their powers.

The appeal panel cannot:

- attach any conditions if it allows your appeal;
- hear complaints or wider objections about local admission policies and practice;
- make the admission authority change your position on the waiting list for the school.

The Local Government Ombudsman has ruled as maladministration, cases in which appeal panels have attached conditions to the offer of a place. The panel has no right to do so. One case involved what might appear to be a sensible caveat – that the place was conditional on the parent being able to show that they had exchanged contracts on a house in the catchment area. In the Ombudsman's ruling it was noted that nothing in the legislation gives the panel the right to set conditions.

The appeal panel can only:

- reject your appeal, or
- make a binding instruction that the admission authority must admit your child.

Who sits on the panel?

The panel of three (most common) or five (rare) members comprises two categories of member: lay members, and members with experience in education. There is a slight difference in eligibility to serve on a panel between panels that will decide about appeals for Community and VC schools (where the Local Authority is the admission authority) and those schools for which their governing bodies are the admission authority (VA and Foundation schools). The differences are minor in nature and do not affect your appeal.

The Code of Practice defines the two categories of panel members as follows:

- *Lay members:* people without personal experience in the management of any school or the provision of education in any school (disregarding experience as a school governor or in any other voluntary capacity). There must be at least one lay member on a panel.
- *Members with experience in education:* people who have experience in education, who are acquainted with educational conditions in the area, or who are parents of registered pupils at a school. There must be at least one member from this category.

Lay members may be governors of other schools as long as those schools are not likely to be involved in the appeal – for example, one at which your child has been offered a place. Good practice is that if governors are used – and many are – then those who serve on secondary-school governing bodies should only hear primary-school appeals, and vice versa. That way there is less chance of a conflict of interest.

Other typical members will include Justices of the Peace, trade-union members, and anyone with experience of hearing appeals (e.g. immigration appeals, industrial tribunals, etc.).

Members from what might be described as 'the professional category' can be drawn from a wide range of people, including parents and teachers. The use of teachers on appeal panels is controversial, although the guide makes it clear that it is permitted as long as the teacher has no involvement with any school that is likely to be mentioned in the appeal. Other members may include retired teachers and Headteachers.

LEGAL POINT

The following people are disqualified from membership of an appeal panel arranged by a governing body (or jointly with other governing bodies):

- *any member of the school's maintaining LEA (i.e. Councillors) or the governing body or bodies in question;*
- *anyone, other than a teacher, employed by the LEA or the governing body or bodies;*
- *any person who has, or has ever had, any connection with the school's maintaining LEA or the school itself, or with any employee of the LEA or the governing body (other than a teacher), such that doubts might be reasonably raised over his or her ability to act impartially regarding the LEA or the school. Employment by the LEA as a teacher is not in itself a reason for disqualifying someone from membership – unless there is another reason to call into question their ability to act impartially – but a person who is a teacher at the school which is the subject of the appeal cannot be a panel member;*
- *no one may be member of an appeal panel if he or she was party to the decision not to admit the child about whom the appeal is concerned, or took part in any discussions about how that decision was reached.*

School Admission Appeals Code of Practice, paragraph 3.3

Included in the documents you received with the admission authority's case should have been a notice of who will be sitting on the appeal panel. This is advisory only; it is not uncommon for panel members to change at the last minute, and if the panel does change at the last minute this does not affect the validity of the hearing. What *would* affect the legality of the hearing is if the panel were not three- or five-strong. There have been cases where one member was not available for an afternoon and the hearings went ahead with only two members present. This was ruled to be maladministration.

All members of the panel should have undergone training. There have been very occasional cases where it has been discovered that panel members have not had appropriate training. Needless to say, the Local Government Ombudsman takes a fairly dim view of panels with untrained members.

The panel should have appointed a chair before the hearings begin. The chair has specific duties and responsibilities during the hearing.

The Ombudsman has criticised panels that appointed their chair on the day of the hearing. The Code of Practice lists the sort of people who make good chairs (paragraph 4.24): experience as a magistrate, committee chair, senior union official or the like is invaluable. He or she has a difficult task ahead of them, one that requires tact and firmness. They must ensure that the hearing is conducted according to the law, but at the same time try and give the proceedings as relaxed a feel as possible so as not to further intimidate already anxious parents.

There is no maximum time for which a member can serve on a panel, and it is a task that requires both experience and a good understanding of the law. However, it is not recommended that members serve on any one panel for more than a few years, for fear that the panel 'goes native' and starts to identify too closely with the admission authority. This is of particular concern to Foundation or VA schools, which are responsible for drawing up their own panels and may have call on only a few trained people, whereas a Local Authority is likely to have a much larger pool from which it can draw. The Code of Practice suggests that panel members only serve 'for a few years' and recommends that neighbouring admission authorities could pool trained panel members. This is good practice and is becoming more widespread.

If you know any of the panel, you must report this straightaway so that a new panel can be drawn up. It would be wrong for any panel member to know the appellant.

How this helps you

You get the panel you get, so there is not a great deal of point worrying too much about it. It *is* worth talking to other parents and asking around if anyone knows anything about the members of your panel. Find out what sort of people they are. What were other people's experiences? What worked for them? Was there anything that seemed to go down well, or indeed badly? The more you can find out about the people who will make the decisions, the more it will help you.

The clerk to the appeal

Every panel must have a clerk. He or she is responsible for coordinating the papers, organising the day and providing legal advice during the appeal itself. Although not a member of the panel – they don't have any role in making the decisions – nonetheless they are an important part of the proceedings. If you wish to submit late papers, etc. then it should be done through the clerk.

LEGAL POINT
The clerk's key tasks are to:

- *explain the basic procedures to appellants and deal with any questions they may have;*
- *ensure that the relevant facts, as provided by both the appellant and the admission authority, are presented and recorded – e.g. where there is an inexperienced chairperson, the clerk might tactfully intervene to assist the panel or parents with procedure;*
- *order the business;*
- *be an independent source of advice on procedure, the Codes of Practice and the law on admissions (usually giving any advice in the presence of the parties to the appeal);*
- *record the proceedings, decisions and reasons; and*
- *notify all parties of the panel's decision.*
  School Admission Appeals Code of Practice, paragraph 4.22

There have been cases of appeals taking place without a clerk present. This is contrary to the Admission Appeals Code of Practice and would amount to maladministration. No appeal can be heard without a clerk.

Should you take anyone with you?

You are perfectly within your rights to take anyone along with you (within reason) and it is a good idea to take someone, even if they are only there to provide support. If your partner or child's other parent is able to attend, it makes a good impression and allows the panel to get a fuller picture of your child. If your partner is not available, or if you are a single parent, this won't work against you – but it is still a good idea to bring along a companion. Don't underestimate how stressful the whole process is. You will want a friendly face there with you.

Some parents consider taking a solicitor with them. This is generally not recommended. For one thing, unless your solicitor has experience of admission appeals and is familiar with the law, their legal knowledge may not be of much use. For another, most appeal members will tell you that having a solicitor present can work against you. Appeal hearings are, by their nature, formal proceedings, but panels will try their hardest to make things as easy as possible for the parent. Although by law they are required to be unbiased, most panels recognise that parents are at a major disadvantage in the appeal – having had no training and only an outline of what to expect, and being far more emotionally involved in the proceedings. After all, it is their child's future that is under discussion. Therefore panels will usually be very lenient on parents, giving them the benefit of the doubt, and allowing them much more leeway than the admission authority.

However, if you bring a solicitor along, that leeway will go. If you have a professional on your side then they will be treated as such. By and large panels do not like solicitors to be present: according to most panel members, they tend to formalise the proceedings, slow things down and bring an overly legalistic approach to the problem.

If, however, you really want to bring along a solicitor, do make sure that they have experience of admission appeals hearings, and have a good understanding of education law. Contact the Education Law Association (http://www.educationlawassociation.org.uk/) or call on 01303 211570. The Education Law service does not operate an advice line; however, it can put you in touch with educational lawyers, child and parent advocates, and voluntary organisations that may be able to advise you.

If you are going to bring along a representative you should notify the clerk to the appeal panel ahead of the meeting.

You may wish to bring witnesses to the hearing to speak on your behalf. Again, if you do, then you must notify the clerk before the hearing. It is unlikely that you would need a witness to be there in person. As has been covered, you will probably wish to have a statement from a witness who can support your appeal, either by bringing factual evidence to the hearing or by providing a character reference for your child, but it is not usual for the witness to attend hearings. Panels may consider it appropriate to allow witnesses who do attend to give evidence, provided that it is relevant and not just a repeat of information they have already heard.

If you do bring a witness, it is up to the panel if they allow the witness to remain in the hearing after they have given evidence.

On the day of the hearing

You should dress in a reasonably smart way for the appeal. The best way to view the appeal is to take it much as you would a job interview, and the panel as you would an employer for whom you would like to work. It does not have to be a suit-and-tie affair, but you should be smart and presentable. Your aim is to make as favourable an impression as possible. Panel members are only human, and as soon as you walk in the door they are going to start to form opinions about you. If you are well dressed and polite, that can only help. If you are scruffy and aggressive then you risk putting them off.

With luck you will already have had a chance to check out the route to the appeal hearing a couple of days earlier. Do make sure you leave yourself plenty of time to get there. If the unthinkable happens and you are delayed, phone the contact number immediately and warn them. If yours is the only appeal hearing, there is a chance they will wait for you. If yours is one of many appeals that day then they may be able to reschedule you later on, but this is by no means certain. And the panel is quite within its rights to hear your appeal without you being present, in which case it will make its decision entirely on the written case you submitted (a good reason to make your written case as thorough as possible).

You should aim to arrive about 5–10 minutes before your appeal is to be heard. Give yourself time to compose yourself, gather your thoughts and make sure you are prepared.

What should be provided:
- *there should be room to allow parties and their representative or adviser to have private discussions;*
- *there should be arrangements (such as a notice on the door) to ensure that the hearing is not interrupted;*
- *the location of the room should not be such that there is likely to be disturbance from noise going on outside;*
- *it is particularly important that those waiting outside should not be able to hear what is going on inside;*
- *the room layout for the appeal hearing should ensure structure, comfort and informality;*
- *drinking water or other refreshments should be available;*
- *toilets should be conveniently located;*
- *there should be name plates for the panel and the clerk;*
- *adequate time should be allowed for the hearing, especially if an interpreter is present to act on behalf of the parents.*
    School Admission Appeals Code of Practice, paragraph 4.13

Who will be there?

Aside from the members of the panel and the clerk, the only other person who must be at the hearing is a representative from the admission authority, there to make the authority's case. In the hearing this person is known as the 'presenting officer'. Rarely there may be other people attending, for example an observer; this may be someone from the Council on Tribunals (the body that has a supervisory role in appeals) or it may be someone who is training to be a panel member, appeal clerk or a Local Authority officer. The chair should introduce everyone in the room to you and explain their role. If you object to an observer being present, you should mention it straightaway.

The admission authority must send a presenting officer. They cannot simply send their written statement. Different admission authorities use different people to present the case. Local Authorities may well have an official whose job includes presenting appeal cases; that person may be supported by the Headteacher of the school, although given the adversarial nature of the hearing, it is not always a good idea to put the Headteacher up against someone who could turn out to be a parent at the school. If you are applying to a VA or Foundation school then the presenting officer will most likely be the chair of the admission committee – although once again, Headteachers sometimes also attend.

CASE STUDY
Mr S and Mrs K appealed against a decision not to admit their child to a Foundation primary school. The governing body, as the admission authority, was required to send a presenting officer but failed to do so, saying that the written case was sufficient. As a result, the hearing was rescheduled and the chair of the panel wrote a strong letter of complaint to the governing body about its attitude. A presenting officer attended the next hearing.

Whomsoever represents the admission authority, they should not have been party to any private knowledge of your case. One appeal went to the Ombudsman after a Local Authority official had helped a group of parents prepare their case, only for those parents to discover on the day of their appeal that the very same person who had been helping them prepare was there to represent the Local Authority against them. This was flagrantly against the principles of natural justice.

When you arrive, the presenting officer should *not* be in the room with the panel unless conducting a hearing. Like you, he or she should be outside, waiting to be called into the hearing by either the clerk or the chair. The Code of Practice is quite insistent that nothing should be done by the panel or by the presenting officer to call into doubt the independence of the panel. Were the presenting officer to be in the room, chatting to the panel, parents would quite rightly feel that they were not being treated as equals.

Furthermore, at no time should the panel be addressed by the presenting officer without you being there. There have been cases of panels receiving briefs by Headteachers, governors and Local Authority officials about the school, or about each case, without the parents being present. This is wholly wrong and has often been criticised by the Local Government Ombudsman.

The order of the hearing

Although the hearing will have a formal feel to it, you should not be alarmed; panels will be sympathetic to your plight. Good panel members understand the parent's anxiety and appreciate the position you find yourself in. One panel member pointed out: 'The only person in the room without any training is the one person who has the most to lose.' With that in mind, a well-run panel will go out of its way to put you at ease.

The appeal panel's work has two phases: the factual stage, during which it must reach a judgement on whether the admission authority carried out its job properly, and whether prejudice exists; and the 'balancing stage' (see also pp. 89–92). (*Note*: appeals against infant class size prejudice follow a slightly different pattern, and will be covered in Chapter 8. Some admission authorities may conduct multiple appeals slightly differently – again see Chapter 8.)

There is no statutory guidance on the order of the hearing, but it is likely to go as follows:

1 *Introduction and welcome by the chair.* The chair should introduce everyone in the room, explain the proceedings and go over any final instructions.
2 *The case for the admission authority.* The presenting officer will make the admission authority's case as to why your child should not be admitted. This should be more than just a re-iteration of their written case, providing more detail. However, new evidence cannot be introduced at this stage.
3 *Questions to the admission authority.* The panel may have questions it wishes to be cleared up. You should certainly have questions to ask; this is one of the key phases of the appeal for you.
4 *The case for the appellant.* You present your case as to why the needs of your child outweigh any problems that the school may suffer.
5 *Questions to the appellant.* You should be prepared to be questioned by both the panel and the presenting officer.
6 *Summing up by the presenting officer.*
7 *Summing up by the appellant.*

As a courtesy to everyone in the room, you should not interrupt anyone when they are speaking. Allow them to finish before talking. It is a good idea to take a notebook and pen in with you to make notes of points you wish to raise, or questions that may occur to you.

When the hearing is over, you and the representatives of the admission authority should leave the room at the same time.

When everyone is out of the room, the panel will make its mind up. As it is not a criminal court, the burden of proof is not so onerous. In court, a jury must be sure 'beyond a reasonable doubt' of the case before they will find someone guilty. In an appeal hearing, the panel is only required to make its ruling based on 'the balance of probabilities'. In other words, you only need to show that broadly speaking, something is likely to be true – and that is sufficient. You do not have to prove it conclusively.

Submission of late documents

In an ideal world, all documents would be presented in advance so that all sides could read and study them ahead of the hearing. However, that is not always possible. So what happens if you need to submit documents at the hearing itself?

It is not generally recommended, but most panels will take a lenient view of parents submitting new documents. The Code of Practice does allow it, although only for parents, in recognition of the fact that they may have had only seven days' notice in which to prepare their appeal. The same is not true of the admission authority, which really has little reason to admit new evidence at the hearing.

LEGAL POINT

If any of the parties wish to raise matters or produce documents at the hearing which are not covered by the statement of decision or the notice of the appeal, these should be submitted to the clerk to the appeal panel in good time before the hearing. If substantial new issues are raised for the first time at the hearing by either the admission authority or the parent, an adjournment may be necessary to allow any party taken by surprise to consider the issues. However, there should be no grounds for the admission authority to produce substantial new information at the appeal, although this should not be true of parents who may only have received the detailed information on which to base their appeal seven days before the hearing.
School Admission Appeals Code of Practice, paragraph 4.32

If you are going to submit late information – and in the next chapter we will look at why and how that might be useful to your appeal – then do remember to bring enough copies for everyone present, including the clerk. You will need around six or seven copies of everything.

How this helps you
Too many parents convince themselves, on no evidence whatsoever, that somehow the hearing is a 'stitch up'. It is not. The panel is

independent of the admission authority, and you must believe that this is so.

Do not be afraid to ask questions of anyone in the room if you don't understand something, or want something clarified. You only get one chance: do not blow it by being afraid to speak up. Good panels will recognise the stress and anxiety that all parents will suffer in the hearing and you will certainly not be penalised for asking.

If at any time during the hearing you need time to think, if you are taken by surprise by any information given, or if you need to compose yourself, you can ask for a short break.

Tread carefully so as not to antagonise the panel. Its members really are there to help you make the most of your case. They may well ask searching questions of the presenting officer. They will have had a lot of experience and are likely to have heard many appeals, so will know the kind of questions to ask. Taking a confrontational approach with the panel is not wise – after all, panel members are only human and if you push them too hard you may well lose their sympathy.

CHAPTER 5

The hearing – part 1

Your strategy is to win a place for your child – and that is all.
The 6Ps. How to question the presenting officer. Is the school
breaking the law? Testing the admission authority's claim to
have correctly implemented their admission criteria

The appeal hearing will open with the admission authority's statement, as the presenting officer lays down, in detail, why your child could not be admitted to the school. Nothing the presenting officer says should be entirely new to you, but it is quite likely that he or she will be able to provide more information and explain in greater detail how the authority reached its decision.

Without a doubt, one of the main reasons that many parents lose their appeal is their failure to question the admission authority's case. All too often, the presenting officer makes his or her statement, the panel asks one or two questions, and that is that. Parents say nothing. To allow the admission authority to get away without being cross-questioned is to allow one of your main attacks to be thwarted before the hearing has really started.

If you can show that what the admission authority believes to be a rock-solid case is in fact anything but, if you can plant the seeds of doubt in the mind of the appeal panel that perhaps the criteria were not applied properly, or maybe the school is not actually full at all, then you stand a good chance of winning. And remember, the burden of proof necessary at the hearing is 'on the balance of probabilities' and not 'beyond a reasonable doubt'. In other words, all you have to show is that the authority could have made a mistake; not that it did, but that it might have – and that could be enough to win the case.

Your strategy is to win a place for your child – and that is all

It sounds cynical to say this, but your aim is not to uncover the truth, nor to find out how the admission authority conducts its business. You are not there on a mission; you are not there as a champion of the underdog. You have one simple aim: to win a place for your child. That is the beginning, middle and end of your strategy. And much as it may sound like 'working the system', anything you can do to help you achieve your aim, while of course remaining inside the law, is fair game.

Your written appeal – which will already be in the hands, and you hope minds, of the panel – should have been written to address the three phases of the appeal:

1 Were the rules correctly applied?
2 Is the school full?
3 Who will suffer most – the school, if my child is offered a place, or my child if he or she is denied one?

> **CASE STUDY**
> Mr and Mrs R appealed against the decision by a rural Foundation secondary school not to offer their son a place on distance grounds. At the hearing, the admission authority produced a map that they claimed showed the addresses of successful candidates. The admission authority's map was incorrect, and as residents of the village, Mr and Mrs R were able to point out where the candidates actually lived. The panel was not confident that the admission authority had correctly applied its own criteria. The appeal was upheld.

In the hearing, your strategy is to reinforce your written case while at the same time doing as much as you can to find fault with, undermine, and generally pick holes in the case for the admission authority. The more you can show that they have not done their job properly, the better your chances.

The School Admission Appeals Code of Practice says that it is not enough to show that a mistake has been made; you must show that the mistake was such that had it not happened, your child would have been offered a place. While that may well be the 'gold standard' – and if you can show that, you are almost certain to win – even if your child was not denied a place as a result of the error, you should none-theless draw the panel's attention to it. If you can show a general pattern of carelessness and mistakes, it may be enough to tip the balance of probability in your favour.

There is an old legal adage that says a barrister should 'never ask a question to which they don't already know the answer'. That may be asking a bit too much of you at the hearing, but you do need to think in advance about the sort of questions you want to ask of the presenting officer, and the sort of answers you want to receive.

LEGAL POINT

The officer should be prepared to answer detailed questions about the case being heard and questions about the school and its admission arrangements, and will need to be present throughout the hearing to be able to do so ... There should be no grounds for the admission authority to introduce substantial new information at the appeal ... If an admission authority has either refused or been unable to provide information requested by an appellant, the panel should decide whether the information is necessary for the hearing to proceed. An admission authority's failure to provide reasonable information should not be allowed to prejudice the child's case, and the panel may choose either to continue or, if they consider it necessary, to adjourn until the information has been provided.

School Admission Appeals Code of Practice,
paragraphs 4.27 and 4.32

The 6Ps

The 6Ps is a phrase borrowed from the military, and stands for 'Prior Preparation and Planning Prevents Poor Performance' (actually, as you might imagine, the military have a seventh, four-letter word beginning with P before the word 'Poor'!). In other words, don't leave things to chance. Thinking up questions for the presenting officer should not be left to the day of the hearing, when you will be under some stress and pressure. Depending on how you react to that pressure, your brain may not be functioning as well as you would like: you could forget to ask questions, you could miss opportunities, and nerves could simply grip you and blow the whole thing. Much better to prepare your questions in advance so you have a pretty good idea of the sort of things you want to ask, and when. You should also try to think about what the presenting officer is likely to answer and plan accordingly, so that you have alternative strategies at the ready.

How does this work in practice? Let's take a fictitious case. Your child has been turned down. The admission criteria are very straightforward – the sibling rule, and distance from the school as measured along safe routes. You believe that they have missed a route, along, say, the High Street and left into Main Road. You have evidence showing that this route is shorter than the normal route. A sensible question to ask would be: 'Did you consider the route along the High Street and left into Main Road?' There are two possible outcomes to this: either the admission authority did, or it did not. You need to consider both outcomes. Your notes would be something along the lines of:

Authority did not consider this route:
Point it out on the map, explain that it is lit along its entire route, etc.

Authority did consider the route:
Question the presenting officer on why it was rejected, etc.

There is another case, where the admission authority's written argument did not provide any detail about the nature of the prejudice that would be caused. The parent had a plan to cover the eventuality that the case for prejudice was brought up for the first time at the hearing, and the eventuality that it was not covered at all. If the authority brought the information up at the hearing, the parent could undermine the authority because of their failure to follow the statutory guidance. If they didn't bring it up at all in their written statement, then the parent had a series of questions prepared for the cross-questioning. Their notes would go something like this:

Did the presenting officer's case cover the exact prejudice that would occur?

Yes:
Why was this information not included in the school's written submission? Why have we had to wait until now to hear this?

No:
I note under the terms of the Code of Practice that, 'It is not enough for the admission authority to show that the admission number has been reached ...'
I also note that under the Code of Practice we should have received 'a written statement summarising the reasons for the decision ...'
Despite it being a requirement in the Code of Practice, there was nothing in the written statement we received from the school that gave any information at all as to why or how admitting our son would 'prejudice the provision of efficient education or the efficient use of resources'. So we will need to cover this now ...

And so on. You can't script the entire meeting, of course, but try to think ahead. That way, you are better prepared, and less likely to be taken by surprise.

How to question the presenting officer

The Local Government Ombudsman has repeatedly criticised admission authorities for not providing adequate statements. In Chapter 3 we saw the checklist of what a statement should contain (see pp. 40–3). Alas, too many authorities fall far short of this ideal, and it will be by questioning that you will be able to tease out the facts that you need to win your case.

There are some almost guaranteed 'get out of jail free' cards – arguments that, if you can prove them on the balance of probabilities, are sufficiently powerful to give you a very, very good chance of winning your appeal. We have already covered some of these, but let's look at them here in more detail:

Is the school breaking the law?

School admissions are bound by many laws, not just those relating to admissions, but also to human rights, equal opportunities, etc. The School Admission Appeals Code of Practice lists the main Acts that admission authorities must be mindful of:

- The Sex Discrimination Act 1975 makes it unlawful for admission policies to discriminate against children on the grounds of sex, except where the school is a single-sex school.
- The Race Relations Act 1976 (as amended by the Race Relations [Amendment] Act 2000) makes it unlawful for admission authorities to discriminate against children on the basis of race, colour, nationality or national or ethnic origin.
- The Disability Discrimination Act 1995 – since September 2002, Part IV of the Disability Discrimination Act 1995 (inserted by the Special Educational Needs and Disability Act 2001) has applied with regard to access to education. Schools and Local Authorities must not treat disabled children less favourably than other pupils for a reason relating to their disability.
- The Human Rights Act 1998 – bodies that carry out a public function, which includes appeal panels, must carry out their functions and duties in accordance with the European Convention on Human Rights. Parents are entitled to a fair hearing by an independent and impartial tribunal.

It is extremely uncommon for admission authorities to fall foul of the race relations and sex discrimination acts. It is conceivable that a misguided admission authority might attempt to balance the sexes in a class and therefore give favourable treatment to one or other sex,

but if it has happened it has not been reported. It is equally conceivable that an admission authority might attempt to conduct such
an exercise with regard to ethnic origin, and certainly any attempt at
discrimination, either positive or negative, would be illegal. Again, if
there have been cases, these have not been widely reported.

That is not to say that race and sex discrimination cases do not
exist, but that they tend to fall outside of the realm of admission
appeals. The Schools Adjudicator, an office established to rule on the
fairness of school admission policies (not appeals), has ruled against
schools on the grounds of unintentional discrimination. For example,
some schools have included in their admission criteria, a preference
for children of old pupils. This has been ruled indirect discrimination
as the effect of such a criterion is likely to act against children from
minority ethnic groups. Likewise, some schools have criteria that give
preference to teachers, and this too can give rise to charges of
indirect racism.

Admission authorities are required to consult on their admission
criteria, but the process and how you raise objections are outside of
the scope of this book. Contact your Local Authority for more
information.

The Disability Discrimination Act (DDA) and the Human Rights Act
(HRA) have both been used in a few appeals:

Human rights

This is a very new area, and conflicts between the rights enshrined in
the HRA and those of pre-existing legislation are continuously being
resolved. The HRA confers a right to education, although this right
does not extend to securing a place at a particular school. Admission
authorities and appeal panels, when respectively considering
applications for admission and appeals against refusals to admit,
should take into account – so far as is compatible with the provision of
efficient instruction and the avoidance of unreasonable public
expenditure – the right of parents to ensure that their child's education
conforms with their own religious or philosophical convictions, as
expressed in any stated reasons for preferring a particular school.

Case law does exist where claims based on the HRA have been
successfully pursued through the High Court. However, this is a very
contentious area. In order to successfully pursue such a claim you
would have to establish a strong case for your beliefs. The Human
Rights Act is based upon the European Convention on Human Rights
and there have been cases in Europe that have been germane:

Belgium: the European Court ruled that French-speaking parents who
lived in the Flemish area of the country were not entitled to have

French-speaking schools provided for them rather than Flemish ones. *Germany:* Parents of a young child had no right to insist on a particular way of teaching maths.

UK: Parents could not insist on a single-sex grammar school for their daughter. The court did not accept their argument that the 'negative ethos' of a comprehensive school went against their convictions.

LEGAL POINT
In a landmark case, Mr K, a devout Muslim, wanted his daughter Z to attend a single-sex school. But instead, the London Borough of Newham offered her a place at a co-educational school. Mr K challenged the decision. The Human Rights Act provides a right to education and a right to respect for religious and philosophical convictions. The High Court decided that Newham had failed to take account of Mr K's religious convictions when deciding whether to offer his daughter a place at their school of choice, and overturned the appeal panel's ruling.

Disability

The DDA defines a 'disabled person' as a person with 'a physical or mental impairment that has a substantial and long-term adverse effect on his or her ability to carry out normal day-to-day activities'. This means that: the person must have an impairment, either physical or mental; the impairment must have adverse effects which are substantial; the substantial effects must be long-term; and the long-term substantial effects must be adverse effects on normal day-to-day activities.

Admission authorities and schools must make reasonable adjustments to ensure that disabled pupils are not placed at a substantial disadvantage compared with non-disabled children. They must not discriminate against a disabled child in the arrangements made for determining admission to the school; in the terms on which they offer admission; and by refusing or deliberately omitting to accept an application for admission.

We have looked at the special circumstances surrounding children with special educational needs (see pp. 18–19). Children who have a disability, but not necessarily severely enough to be classified as special needs, can appeal through one of two routes: the normal school admission appeals process, or the Special Educational Needs and Disability Tribunal (SENDIST). The processes and timescales are quite different, so it is worth contacting your local SENDIST (ask the Local Authority for details) as soon as you are notified that your child has not been awarded a place, if you believe that your child's disability may have played any part in the decision.

If you do go down the regular school admission appeals process, then a successful claim would have to be based on identifying *how* the admission authority discriminated against your child. The panel would have to consider if:

- the reason for the exclusion relates to the child's disability;
- it was less favourable treatment than someone would get if they were not disabled;
- the less favourable treatment could not be justified.

If you did not mention on your application form that your child had a disability then it may have a bearing on your case. The admission authority can only go on the evidence it had at the time. However, the appeal hearing can, and will, take your child's disability into account.

If you are the parent of a child with a disability, then even if you can't establish a case of discrimination, you may well be able to establish a strong case under the balancing stage of the appeal. If you can show that you and/or your child will be genuinely put out and will truly suffer because of the admission authority's refusal to offer you a place, that would be a strong argument.

If you believe that your child has been discriminated against on the basis of disability, then get in touch with the Disability Rights Commission, which has oversight of the legislation and will be able to offer advice and guidance. Appeals under the DDA would take the form of formal legal proceedings.

Questions to ask

✔ How many pupils with disabilities have been admitted to the school?

✔ How many pupils with disabilities have applied to the school but been refused admission? If you can show a pattern that the admission authority has several times refused places to disabled children, then you could establish a case for discrimination. To defend against such a charge, the school would have to be able to show that the refusal to admit these children was based on their published admission criteria.

✔ Was the child with disability treated less favourably than a child without disability? And if so, was there a reasonable justification for such treatment? If there was no justification, or the panel felt that the justification was not reasonable, then it may well be that the decision not to offer your child was illegal. If the panel felt that the decision was justifiable then the decision would be legal.

Ultimately, the only authority that can give a definite ruling on the legality of a decision is a court.

How this helps you

Since the Newham judgement, religious or philosophical beliefs should be considered by a panel. If you can provide well-founded evidence, you may have a case. It is worth noting that the panel can, and should, challenge you hard to test the authenticity of your claims.

If you are the parent of a child with disabilities then you should make sure that there has not been any discrimination against your child, even indirectly or inadvertently. Such discrimination is illegal and panels have been instructed in court rulings to disregard criteria that are illegally enforced.

Signs that you may not have a case

✗ If the admission authority can show that your child's disability was unrelated to their decision not to admit (for example, you lived too far away, or failed to match other criteria).

Testing the admission authority's claim to have correctly implemented their admission criteria

To prove successfully that a mistake was made in applying the admission criteria to your child, you need to show that a child who had an equal, or lesser, claim to a place than your own child was admitted, while your child was not. The key to this is the way in which the rules were written and implemented. Some criteria are pass-or-fail tests – either you have a sibling at the school at the time of application, or you don't (as long as the word 'sibling' has been defined). Either you live in the defined catchment area, or you don't.

But other criteria can be not quite so black and white. Given that each of the 32,000 schools in the country has its own admission criteria, it is impossible to give specific advice. However, there are two common problem areas that we have already looked at, and which we can cover in more detail here: the faith test for schools of a religious character, and distance measurements.

Faith schools

In Chapter 1 we looked at how some poorly worded criteria can cause problems. We'll look now at how to test the criteria and the way in which they were applied to your child.

The Code of Practice says that whatever admission criteria an authority adopts, they must be clearly defined and objectively assessable (paragraph 3.6). There can be a problem for faith-based schools in reconciling evidence of strength of belief with an objective test. For example, some schools may use a phrase like 'children whose parent(s) are committed Christians worshipping regularly'. Such a phrase may seem to be quite straightforward: if you go to church, your child will get in. But what does 'committed Christian' mean? What does 'regularly' mean? How will these be tested? As we have already seen, the most common test is a letter from a priest or minister. However, you may well be able to challenge the way in which the decision was made.

For instance, the Local Government Ombudsman has criticised admission authorities that try to test levels of commitment by pitting one parent against another in a sort of 'holier than thou' approach. Whatever test is used, it must be subjective and must be clearly indicated in the admission criteria. So it would be legitimate to ask the admission authority how they determined levels of commitment. If someone failed to attend Sunday services, was that due to lack of commitment, or was it due to other family circumstances – such as work?

One Catholic girls school gave a list of published admission criteria and then stated that 'priority will be given to those who express a desire for a Catholic education first and foremost'. Such a statement is potentially difficult. How do you express such a desire? Who is to judge it, and by what measure? Is this some kind of 'beauty contest' in which one parent's claim is measured against another's? Such contests have been criticised by the Ombudsman.

Faced with such phrases you should seek to question the presenting authority in some detail. Ask them to explain exactly how these tests were conducted and by whom. Ask them to show in the published admission criteria the details of the tests (remember, the School Admissions Code of Practice requires any criteria to be clearly defined and objective – ask them what were the objective measures). Your aim is to show that your child has been unfairly ruled-out because the testing regime was open to too much personal inter-pretation by the committee and as such the ruling was arbitrary.

A more tightly phrased criterion leaves less room for manoeuvre. A phrase such as 'children who are stated by their parish priest to be practising Catholics, defined as weekly attendance at Sunday Mass' is objective and clearly defined. Does the priest say that your child attends Mass weekly? Either they do, or they don't – although there is some very small 'wriggle room'. If you could support it, you might produce an argument to show *why* you could not attend every week. (In fact, the second priority of the school in question allowed for that, stipulating that second priority went to baptised Catholics stated by their parish priest to attend at least once a month.)

CASE STUDY
An urban Catholic primary school required parents to demonstrate their commitment to the church, and included a question-
naire to measure their degree of Catholicism. Ms J was marked
down because her child had not been baptised within a year of
birth and she was not married to the father of the child. The
appeal panel felt that this was an unreasonable interpretation of
the guidance. The appeal was upheld. Under future legislation,
admission authorities may not make decisions based on the
marital status of the parents.

Questions to ask
✔ How is the level of faith measured, by whom and on what basis?
✔ Is the test clear from the published admission criteria?
✔ How much room for interpretation was given? Was allowance
made for non-attendance due to work or serious family commit-
ments?

How this helps you
If you can show that the tests for commitment are subjective, and if
you can show that your application was at least as good as that of
other successful candidates, then you have a strong case. Even if you
can't, perhaps you can show that the admission authority made an
arbitrary decision against you that was not based on subjective
grounds, but on someone expressing their opinion. If so, you may be
successful.

Signs that you may not have a case
✘ The criteria are well phrased with clear yes/no answers.
✘ Tests are objectively assessable, and the only accepted evidence is
a letter from an established religious figure certifying your attendance and/or commitment.

Distance from school
We have examined the problems with distance in Chapter 1. But the
hearing itself will be your first chance to question the presenting
officer about how exactly the distance was measured.

The admission authority should specify in its submission what
measuring system it used to make the decision based on distance,
what that distance was, where the 'cut-off' point was (in other words,
the distance to the last successful child), and to what point at the
school they measured it.

Before the appeal hearing you should ask for – and the authority should provide you with – a copy of any maps they used to locate your address. Do check that they have correctly identified your house.

There is some confusion about exactly what distance admission authorities should measure. As we have seen, this tends to fall into two camps: straight-line measurement, and measurement along recognised routes. From the point of view of winning your appeal, there is more opportunity if the admission authority does use such an inherently inaccurate system as straight-line measurement. You may well be able to exploit its quite significant errors.

However, a lot of Local Authorities and many schools now use geographic information systems. If this is the case – and the admission authority's statement should state how the distance was measured – then alas, there is not a lot one can do to challenge the distance. Of course you should check it (see Appendix 1 for how to calculate the distance between two points on a map), but unless the wrong address was entered, or there was some mistake in typing in the figures, it is highly unlikely that an error will have been made.

However, if the admission authority only used your postcode and not your full address, then you may be in a position to argue. As we saw in Chapter 1, systems that use only the postcode are liable to introduce error. In a rural setting, where postcodes cover larger areas, that error could be very significant.

Find out from the authority which system they used. There are a number of websites (multimap.com, streetmap.co.uk, etc.) that will show a map of a postmid and give a grid reference to it. Look and see if the spot they mark is your house; is it in fact some distance away?

If it is not made clear in the admission authority's statement how the distance from your address to the school was calculated, then contact the admission authority and ask them. Find out *before* the appeal hearing how it was determined. If they used a geographic information system then challenging them over the calculation is not likely to be fruitful.

CASE STUDY

Mr and Mrs B appealed against a decision not to admit their child to a Foundation secondary school. The school claimed that they were 1mm beyond the last successful candidate. They were able to show that the admission authority had not measured to the right point on their property and to show that the measuring system was not sufficiently accurate to be able to claim millimetre accuracy. Their appeal was upheld.

If they used some other method, you may have more room to manoeuvre. Find out the distance to the last successful candidate – again, it should be in the statement. If not, then ask. If you are tens of millimetres off then you have no case. However, if you are within a few millimetres, examine the case very carefully indeed. Something as simple as putting a pin in a map can introduce a millimetre of error; measuring with a ruler will introduce several millimetres of error; using a postcode system can introduce additional errors, and so on. If you can prove that the errors in the system are greater than the distance between your own house and that of the nearest successful child, then you might have a good argument.

Questions to ask
✔ Why does the admission authority use this system?
✔ How does the admission authority ensure the level of accuracy it is claiming?
✔ What is the error margin in the measurement?
✔ How did the admission authority identify your particular house?
✔ If you think the admission authority may be unsure which is your house, ask them to point out where you live on the map.

How this helps you
It can be decisive if you can show that children who live further from the school than you do were admitted, while your child was denied a place; or if you can show that the system is not sufficiently accurate and so a mistake could have been made that denied your child a place.

Signs that you may not have a case
✗ If the admission authority uses a geographic information system to calculate, rather than measure, distances between home and school. These are usually very accurate.
✗ If you live a long way from the school and the last successful candidate is quite a lot closer.

Safest route to school
A less common test, sometimes found in urban schools where walking to school is the norm. It is more common in primary than secondary schools. A variant on this is recognised route by public transport, or by road route. Some admission authorities recognise that straight-line distance may not be a very fair way of determining who gets in. There may be children who by straight line live very close, but whose journey would take them much further (for example, a railway line or river or canal between their home and school might mean that a long route is needed).

It is helpful if the admission authority has pre-determined routes which they have published – so that there is less scope for argument. The admission authority is quite entitled to do this as long as it specifies the routes in advance and makes maps available. However, even if an authority has pre-determined a route, you can appeal against it if you can find another route that meets their criteria and which they had not considered.

Typically, walking routes should:

- be lit;
- be along safe routes (e.g. not down alleyways, etc.);
- be paved or on recognised pathways;
- avoid major road crossings.

Routes should not:

- rely on unofficial short-cuts (e.g. down back alleys, etc.);
- involve trespass or any route across private land;
- involve crossing traffic except at recognised crossing points, unless traffic is very light.

Successful appeals have been made in which the parents were able to show that a perfectly safe route had not been considered by the admission authority. If you believe you can identify a safe route that would benefit your appeal, it is certainly worth using it.

You will also need to measure the route as accurately as you can. If you can get hold of a measuring wheel – of the type used by surveyors, for example – then that is the most accurate way of measuring. Failing that, get the most detailed scale you can (the Ordnance Survey does 1:5,000 scale maps of urban areas) and measure it via the map. Do not attempt to measure your route on a normal 1:25,000 or 1:50,000 scale map, as they lack the detail. Detailed town maps are often available in your local library.

Be wary of commercial software that calculates distance by driving. First, they are not that precise; and second, unless you specify the exact journey, the road the software chooses may not be the right route.

If all else fails, pace out the various routes yourself and just count the paces.

Questions to ask

✔ What criteria were used to determine the routes chosen?
✔ Were alternative routes considered? If not, why not?
✔ How was the route measured?

Even if the authority says it makes offers based only on its routes, the appeal panel is not bound to follow that restriction. If a perfectly reasonable alternative is offered then the appeal panel can accept it.

How this helps you
There is a bit of leeway in safest recognised route criteria, as they are open to some interpretation in what constitutes a safe route. Furthermore, authorities may not be aware of every route to the school.

Signs that you may not have a case
✘ There are no other routes.
✘ Your alternative route does not match the criteria the admission authority laid down, or would not be considered safe. Even if you can show that it is a common and popular route, if it is unsafe then it is unlikely that the appeal panel will accept it.

CHAPTER 6

The hearing – part 2

Establishing the case for prejudice. Can any more children fit in? Unequal pupil numbers. Provision of efficient education. End of the factual stage. Presenting your case. Use of witnesses. How to deal with questions about your allocated school. The summing up. Leaving the appeal. The ruling

In the last chapter we looked at ways to question the admission authority over its case that the rules were applied correctly. Here we will consider the next part of the appeal. Has the admission authority really shown that the school is full? Has it shown that to admit more children would 'prejudice the provision of efficient education and the efficient use of resources'? If you can show to the satisfaction of the appeal panel that the school is not really full, although it may appear to be, then you will have a strong case.

We will also consider appeals to infant classes, but not the specific case of 'infant class size prejudice' – that is, where an infant class is at the legal maximum number of children allowed (30) and to admit any extra children would force the school to take 'qualifying measures'. This will be dealt with in Chapter 8. Even if your admission authority has said that yours is a case of infant class size prejudice, you should prepare an appeal to deal with normal prejudice. It is possible that the appeal panel may reject the admission authority's case for infant class size prejudice, in which case the special rules will no longer apply.

Establishing the case for prejudice

Since the admission authority is saying that the school is full, what you must show is that although the published admission number may have been reached, the school is *not* full – so that admitting your child will not cause the school the problems it is claiming. To put it another way, you have to show that the published admission number is wrong.

That is quite a tall order. The fact that you are appealing to get your child into the school is an indication of how popular it is. There is a very strong likelihood that the school is full, and that to admit more children would cause problems. You must accept that good schools are oversubscribed and that they are probably operating at capacity.

However, many cases have been won against admission authorities that claimed a school was full when in fact it wasn't. Your aim must be to make the panel believe there is capacity that is being under-used. Let's see how.

Can any more children fit in?

In Chapter 3 we looked at the recommended guidelines for class sizes. If the information on net capacity figures was not included in the admission authority's written statement, you will have to question them at the meeting on the capacity of the classrooms, etc. The Local Government Ombudsman has severely criticised authorities that fail to provide this information.

> *The onus is on the admission authority to convince the appeal panel that the admission of an additional child or children would cause prejudice to efficient education or the efficient use of resources, and that the published admission criteria were correctly applied in refusing a place to the child. An appellant should be able to know the case which the admission authority is going to make and be able to question it. Appellants should therefore know in advance exactly what evidence is going to be put forward to demonstrate the case for the admission authority.*
> *The Commission for Local Administration in England: Special Report School Admissions and Appeals, section E, paragraph 2*

The first thing to consider is the published admission number (PAN). Admission authorities are required to print not only the published admission number – the number of children they will admit – but also the indicated admission number – the number of children that the school can physically hold, calculated according to the government figures.

Is there a difference between the two? If the indicated number is greater than the published number (in other words, the school can take more children than they are admitting) there must be a very good reason for this. The school will have to have consulted on this before setting a published number below its indicated number. Find out why. What reasons did they give? You are looking for anything that will help your claim that the school can take more children than it says it can.

CASE STUDY
Mrs K appealed against a decision to refuse a place to her son at a primary school. The admission number had been set two years ago, but the school had undergone refurbishment and modernisation, with additional classrooms added and several old rooms knocked into one. The admission number had not been updated to reflect the increased capacity. The appeal panel felt that the number was too low and was not justified. Her case was upheld.

Find out when the PAN was set and the last time it was changed. When the new system for calculating admission figures was introduced, many schools ended up with a figure that was exactly the same as their old one, so it may not have changed for many years. If the figure was revised last year, or the year before, then there isn't much to go on; if however, the figure was set some time ago – say, three or four years – then that may be worth investigating.

In order to establish whether or not there is prejudice, the panel will wish to consider a number of factors, such as the school's published admission number and, for applications made for admission to a later year group, whether any changes have been made to the school's physical accommodation or staffing level since an admission number was set for that year group when it was the normal year for admission to the school. The appeal panel should be satisfied that the school's published admission number is a justified limit.
School Admission Appeals Code of Practice, paragraph 4.61

Has there been building work at the school since the PAN was set? If you can establish that additional space has been added to the school, but that the PAN has remained the same, then this may support an argument that the published admission number is too low. A good line of questions to ask the presenting officer would be about the published admission number. When was it set? When was it last revised? Were the new buildings taken into account? Remember to look at the rule-of-thumb figures for assessing net capacities.

If, however, no additional capacity has been added, it will be difficult to argue the point.

How this helps you
If the panel feels that the published admission number is too low, and if you are the only appellant, it will allow your appeal. If you are one of many then it will decide how many more children can be admitted without causing problems. Your child could be one of them.

> *Net capacity does not need to be calculated every year. It will only need to be updated if physical changes are made to the usable space, such as:*
> * *space being removed or more space being added;*
> * *several small spaces being converted into one larger one;*
> * *changes being made that affect the type of space in classbases in primary schools or in teaching spaces in secondary schools.*
>
> *Assessing the Net Capacity of Schools, paragraph 28*

If your presenting officer does not have the information you require, this may help you. An appeal panel can only make its ruling on the information that is presented to it on the day; the panel cannot rule on evidence it has not heard. So, for example, if the presenting officer claims that the classrooms are too small but cannot provide the evidence, then that could work in your favour. Remember that the Code of Practice requires the admission authority to show what prejudice would be caused.

Questions to ask
✔ When was the admission number set?
✔ Has there been additional building work since the number was set?
✔ Is that new work reflected in the admission number? If not, then why not?

Signs that you may not have a case
✘ Take care with these questions. They are only worth raising at the hearing if you know that the PAN hasn't been changed for a while, and that the capacity has gone up. If the admission authority can show that the number has gone up with building work, or that no capacity has been added to the school, then you don't have a case.
✘ The admission authority has admitted a number of children with special educational needs. The net capacity system allows an admission authority to reduce its intake by up to 10% to cater for SEN admissions.
✘ Any admission authority that provides the net capacity figures is going to have done its homework, and the chances are that they will have calculated the capacity of each classroom according to the prescribed formula. If this is the case, there is not much more you can do to question the authority on capacity, and instead will have to concentrate on prejudice of efficient use of resources.

Unequal pupil numbers

It is worth having a look at the numbers of pupils in each year group. If the admission authority has been careful, then the number of pupils in each year will be broadly the same, and will be roughly equal to the published admission number. However, if there are large differences between year groups, then find out why. What you hope to find is a large year group going through the school that is doing well. These figures should be available from the school's prospectus, but remember that the Code of Practice gives you the right to ask the admission authority for anything that will help you.

Armed with this knowledge, ask the presenting officer about that year group and how it is doing. Logically it will be hard for the admission authority to claim that the school will struggle if they admit children over the published admission number if they already have year groups that are over the number and doing well.

Take care, though. The admission authority could argue that such a large group has put a strain on the school's resources and that despite it doing so well, the admission authority cannot allow such a situation to repeat itself.

On the flip side, if there is an unusually small year group, it could indicate unused capacity in the school – a sign that they may be able to admit over the published number in a later year.

Another thing to look for is uneven class sizes. Have a look at the PAN. Divide the PAN by the number of classes in the year of admission. Your answer should be a whole number (for example, a secondary school has a PAN of 324 and 12 classes in Yr 7; that would give a class size of 27). If the figure is not a whole number then you have different class sizes in the same year, which is unusual and may well be worth investigating, for it may give you a useful line on capacity. If a year group is organised with seven classes of 28 and one of 27, then the obvious area to probe is why? What is preventing the school from taking one more child?

How many children do they have in each class? If the number is quite low (say under 25), then find out why. Many primary schools have quite small class sizes so there would be nothing unusual in that, but it would be unusual in a secondary school. If class sizes are small there should be some indication as to why in the admission authority's case. If not, then you will need to probe this at the hearing. Again, tie this in with the net capacity figures to see if the school is underusing its space. If the school has large classrooms with a small number of pupils in them, you may have a good case to challenge on 'the efficient use of resources'.

How this helps you

If a large group is doing well, then that sets a precedent. If the school has coped with a large group before without problems, then it is not unreasonable to suggest that the same could be done again.

Questions to ask

✔ Ask about the large year group. How well are the pupils doing?

✔ How did the school manage to cope with these numbers?

✔ Would it be possible to repeat that experience with another year group?

✔ What strategies has the school used to deal with this large year group? Why could they not be repeated?

Signs that you may not have a case

✘ Take care with these questions. They are only worth raising at the hearing if that year group has done well, or at least maintained the performance of older groups. If the admission authority can show that the large year group has not done well, it may harm your argument.

✘ If the school's year groups are broadly consistent.

Provision of efficient education

The Code of Practice is very clear that the admission authority must not only prove that the school is full, but also show what harm would be caused if more children were admitted. While many authorities are quite good at showing how full they are, they are sometimes not as good at showing the problems that this causes.

> *It is not enough for the admission authority to show that the admission number has been reached; it should also demonstrate what prejudice would be caused by the additional admission.*
> **School Admission Appeals Code of Practice, paragraph 4.61**

The admission authority can use a number of arguments to support its case. For them, the best case is to show a link between rising admissions and falling standards, or to show unreasonable strain on resources, or very unsatisfactory pupil:teacher ratios.

Admission authorities may use a financial argument if you are appealing outside the normal admissions round (see also pp. 23–4). Since school budgets are fixed once a year, to admit a child outside the normal round and after the school census (known as PLASC) is taken (usually in January) would mean that the child would effectively be unfunded for the remainder of the year. That alone may be a sufficient case to argue for prejudice. It would be harder for them to argue this during the normal admission round, since if your child was admitted, the authority would receive funding for him or her in the same way as for any other child in that year.

The admission authority may also point to classroom use at, or very near to, capacity, and limitations on the delivery of the curriculum because of constraints such as science lessons conducted in ordinary classrooms, use of the main hall for PE, and use of specialist areas (such as drama studios, etc.) for ordinary classes. Any evidence that this is widespread would help the authority support its argument that prejudice is occurring and that to admit more children would make the situation worse.

What is clear is that at some point prejudice will occur. What *you* need to show is that admitting your child is not going to be the cause of it.

If a school is claiming prejudice, but has continued to produce good results when oversubscribed, question the presenting officer on how it achieves this. It is not unreasonable to expect that if the school can do it for one year, then it can carry on doing it for another year.

Scan the school's latest Ofsted for any comments about overcrowding. Ofsted inspectors see a huge variety of schools: if they do not mention overcrowding or make any reference to pressure on resources in their report then that is significant – question the presenting officer about it. If overcrowding is an issue at the school, why was no mention made of it in the latest Ofsted report? If new buildings have been opened since an Ofsted report that failed to mention overcrowding, and the admission number has also not increased, then ask the presenting officer why that is the case.

In questioning the presenting officer's case for efficient education, remember that you must try to create doubt in the minds of the panel. Always remember that it is not up to you to prove that prejudice won't happen; it is up to the admission authority to show that it will.

How this helps you

This is a central plank of the appeal system. Admission authorities are required by law not only to prove that their school is full, but also to show that admitting more children will harm the provision for those already at the school. If they can't establish that, then they have no case.

Questions to ask

✔ What evidence is there that admitting more pupils causes problems? And what are those problems?

✔ How have results in the past been affected by increased numbers?

✔ What strategies has the school used to deal with this in the past?
✔ What are the school's pupil:teacher and pupil:adult ratios (see pp. 51–2) and how do these compare with national figures?
✔ Why was overcrowding not mentioned in the latest Ofsted report?

Signs that you may not have a case
✗ The school has struggled in the past to maintain standards.
✗ Unreasonable or excessive demands were placed upon the school in the past.
✗ Any official recognition that overcrowding is causing problems.

End of the factual stage

The first part of the hearing is now complete. The admission authority will have made its case and you will have questioned it – with luck, in some detail. This is a crucial point in the appeal process. Some appeals, typically group appeals (see Chapter 8), may actually break at this point for the panel to consider its judgement. Most, however, do not.

If the panel concludes that the admission authority did not apply its own rules correctly, as a result of which your child was denied a place that he or she would have been granted had they done so, then it must find in your favour.

If the panel concludes that the admission authority did do its job properly, then it must consider if the school is really full or not. If it thinks the school can cope with more children and yours is the only appeal, then it must find in your favour. However, if there are multiple appeals, then the panel must judge each appeal on its own merits and make a comparison between the cases.

The third option is that the panel finds the process was conducted properly and that the school is really full. It will then move to the next stage, the balancing stage. This is a much more contentious area for the panel, as it must make a subjective judgement weighing up your child's needs against those of the school.

A note of realism here. To have reached this stage is for the panel to have agreed that the school is full, and to recognise that there will be issues for the school and the children already attending the school if more children are admitted. Therefore, any case you make must be compelling. You must show that there will be very real problems, not just inconveniences, to you and/or your child if your child does not attend that particular school. This is a tough call.

Most panels move directly from the factual stage to the balancing stage without a break. The panel will only make its consideration once it has heard the whole appeal and you and the presenting officer have left the room. In making its decision it will go through all the stages in order. If the panel concludes that a mistake was made, or that the school is not full, it will not go on to make a judgement about the strength of your case.

Presenting your case

It can seem daunting to be in a room full of strangers and have them cross-question you on your case. For most parents the prospect of being questioned is quite worrying, and most are anxious about their answers: either they will say the wrong thing and undermine their own case, or they will forget to say something important. That is why it is a very good idea to have your case written out, and to have thought about questions you might be asked, and the answers you will give.

The presenting officer is entitled to ask questions, and while many do, it is not unusual to find that most of the questions come from the panel itself. This is no bad thing and you should be as helpful and open as possible. Panels are under quite clear guidance to give the benefit of doubt to the parent, and to recognise the pressures that you will be under.

The appeal panel and the presenting officer will have already read your case and should be familiar with the points you are going to raise. In Chapter 2 we saw how to prepare your case, the sort of information it should contain, and the vital importance of solid evidence to back it up.

When it comes to presenting your case, you don't have to do a lot more than refer the panel to the written case if there is nothing you wish to add. However, this is your opportunity to speak directly to the people who will be deciding on your child's future. It is wise to use it. Even if you simply say something along the lines of, 'You have all read my case. I don't want to waste the panel's time, but I would like to draw your attention to . . .' and then highlight whatever point of your appeal you think is the most noteworthy. That way it will be foremost in their minds when they come to make their judgement.

The Code of Practice does give you – though not the presenting officer – the right to introduce new evidence at this stage. This is a risky strategy. While you have every right to do so, the panel is not compelled to accept any new evidence you may submit; even if it does accept it, if the new information is of a compelling nature, then the presenting officer may call for a break, or an adjournment, to consider it.

It may be tempting to attempt to 'ambush' the appeal by producing a killer piece of evidence which the presenting officer has never seen and which causes his or her case to collapse. If you could pull it off, like in some TV courtroom drama, then it would be a great success. But what happens if the panel ruled that it would not accept the evidence? It would be a disaster. This is not TV. It is much safer to be completely above board and to present all your information before the appeal.

That being said, you may have very good reasons to introduce new evidence even at this late stage. If you have had only seven days to prepare your case, it is quite possible that you may not have had time to gather everything you need – for example, it may take time to get letters from consultants, etc. Panels will be sympathetic to this and would not unreasonably refuse to allow such evidence.

Use of witnesses

You are entitled, with prior warning, to ask a witness to attend the hearing. The use of witnesses at appeals is however uncommon.

> *Parents are entitled to decide how to organise their presentation to the appeal panel but it is unlikely to be necessary for witnesses to attend. The panel may consider it appropriate to allow witnesses who do attend to give evidence, provided that it is relevant and not repetitive. Panels may (with advance warning to the parents) ask for corroboration from them on matters such as medical conditions or the parents' address, etc.*
> *School Admission Appeals Code of Practice, paragraph 4.36*

Before considering asking a witness to attend, think about what they will bring to the hearing by being there in person rather than submitting a written report. If you are planning on asking someone to speak for you on a medical point, could the same information be presented in a letter? Or for social or personal reasons, again, could your witness not present their information in another way?

However, there may be times when that is not the best way of presenting your case, and you may feel that given the complexity of the information, it is best coming directly from an expert. Notify the clerk to the appeal panel in plenty of time. He or she may contact the chair of the panel to get a direction from them.

Make sure you know in advance what your witness is going to say, and brief them on the substance of your case. This is not to suggest that your witness is only going to answer questions that benefit your case, but they should be fully aware of what points you are going to make. If they are not prepared to do that, then it is best not to call them.

You are free to question your own witness, although it is more common for the panel to do so. Your witness should be prepared to answer questions from the presenting officer as well.

When they have finished presenting their evidence to the panel, it will be up to the chair of the panel if your witness remains in the hearing or is asked to leave.

How to deal with questions about your allocated school

If the admission authority is the Local Authority, there is a chance that you could effectively be appealing against a decision not to admit your child to one school, and also against the allocated school. (If you are dealing with a school's governing body – in other words, you are appealing to a VA or Foundation school – this is less relevant.)

Do not fall into the trap of laying into the allocated school. It is very easy to do, but it is not wise – first, because it may make you appear narrow-minded, and second because it could lead you into arguments that you don't need to get into.

Do address the issue of the allocated school, but make your case a factual one. Identify – and make sure you have supporting evidence – any weaknesses in the school. For example, if your child has a particular speciality and that school does not provide for it, then mention this. If you are concerned about behaviour issues, then find evidence from the allocated school's last Ofsted report that supports your case. (If you want to be doubly sure, try and find evidence from Ofsted that says how good the discipline is at the school to which you are appealing.)

If you are questioned about the allocated school then be brief, polite and factual. Try not to be drawn into expressing your opinions about the school, just stick to the facts. It is better to be positive about the school to which you are appealing, than negative about your allocated school. In other words, try and turn questions about the allocated school around, so that instead of talking about that school, you talk about the school you want your child to attend. The chances are that the appeal panel will know the allocated school anyway and will have their own opinions about it.

If you are applying to a VA or Foundation school, the allocated school is of less relevance. Your written appeal should show that you have done your homework in visiting the schools and reading their Ofsted reports. It is unlikely that you will be asked questions about it, though.

The summing-up

Both parties – the presenting officer and the parent(s) – are given the chance to sum up at the end of the hearing. The presenting officer speaks first, which means that the advantage lies with you, the parent. You have the last word in the hearing, so make the most of it.

It is best to have scripted your summing-up in advance, but be ready to add any additional pieces of information that you have learned in the course of the hearing. With luck, that will be quite significant.

Start your summing-up by thanking the panel. This is a simple courtesy, but one that is not often observed. Even if you feel that the whole affair has been the most ghastly experience and you never want to put yourself through anything like it again (rest assured it is unlikely), do thank the panel members. They have a difficult job to do.

There is plenty to be gained by thanking the presenting officer. They too have a difficult job, and while they are your 'opponent' in the appeal, it is not likely to be personal. Many presenting officers find the process very stressful, knowing full well that if they succeed they will be inflicting real disappointment, and even genuine hardship, on you.

Then very briefly go through the main points of the admission authority's case that you dispute, and point out to the panel members the weaknesses that with luck you have exposed through questioning. Highlight the strengths of your case and draw attention to the points that you wish them to take away with them.

It is also worth bringing the whole proceedings slightly down to earth by reminding the hearing what all this is about – your child. Try to personalise your appeal by explaining how much it matters to your child that they get into this particular school. After all, that is what the appeal should be about – the needs of your child.

Finally, use the old trick favoured by politicians when making a speech. Leave the panel on a 'high', so that their final impression of you is a good one. Don't turn your appeal into a slanging match, laying into people; it will leave a very unfortunate final impression. You want the panel to think of you as a reasonable person with a well-thought-out and well-constructed appeal that has addressed all the points in the Code and is logical and coherent. Some may call that 'spin'; others may just think it is about creating the right impression.

Leaving the appeal

The chair should thank you and the presenting officer for your time, and invite the clerk to show you all out at the same time. The presenting officer should not remain in the room after you – nor indeed should you be in the room without the presenting officer present.

And that is it.

What you do after your appeal is up to you. Go for a long walk, go to the pub, go to see friends. Do what you have to do to unwind. When you finally walk out of that room it will bring to an end weeks or even months of worry. Whatever happens now is outside your control.

You have given it your best shot, you have said what you wanted to say, raised the points you wanted to raise and left the panel with a clear understanding of your case. Almost certainly you will think of things you should have said, or questions you should have asked – that is only human nature. But try not to dwell on it.

The ruling

The panel, together with the clerk, will assemble after your hearing to discuss your case. If yours is the only case it must hear, then it will assemble immediately and make a decision there and then. If the panel is hearing more than one appeal then it may make a few comments, but will not discuss your appeal in detail and make a ruling on it until all the appeals have been heard.

When the panel members do meet to discuss your case, they must go through a formal two-stage process: the factual stage and the balancing stage. They will go through both your case and the presenting officer's, using the questions that were asked in the appeal to help them. The clerk may also provide guidance although he or she has no role to play in the actual decision.

Their ruling is a straightforward one: either your appeal is upheld, in which case your child will go to the school, or your appeal is denied, in which case he or she won't. They cannot attach any conditions to their ruling; furthermore the appeal panel's ruling is binding on the admission authority. If the panel finds in your favour and instructs the admission authority to admit your child, the authority must do so.

CHAPTER 7

After the appeal

The panel upholds your appeal. The panel does not uphold your appeal. Waiting lists. Another appeal. Other routes. Appeals to the Secretary of State for Education. Judicial review. Appeals to the Local Government Ombudsman. What constitutes maladministration? How to appeal to the Ombudsman

You should hear back from the appeal panel quite quickly. The Code of Practice says seven days from the appeal, but if yours is one of a group of appeals it can take longer. The letter should come from the clerk to the appeal panel and it must explain exactly the process the panel went through, clearly indicating the various stages of the appeal and the judgement the panel reached. The courts have said that the decision letter must give reasons that enable parents to understand

> *The panel must communicate the decision, and the grounds on which it is made, in writing to parents and the admission authority. The decision letter should make reference to the two-stage process – unless that was not followed, for example because the appeal involved a class size issue – and indicate the establishment of prejudice by the admission authority. The letter should also explain in full why the panel decided that the individual circumstances of the parents' case were considered sufficient or insufficient to outweigh the prejudice arguments of the admission authority, making reference to any other issues raised by the parent which were considered by the panel.*
>
> *The written decision should be sent by the clerk and it should be expressed clearly, using straightforward language that can be readily understood by a lay person. The letter should be sent as soon as possible after the appeal panel has made its decision and ideally within seven days, although this may not always be possible where there are multiple appeals for one school.*
>
> *School Admission Appeals Code of Practice, paragraphs 4.81,4.82*

how the decision has been made. In particular, where a point of crucial significance is raised by an appellant, the letter needs to explain what the panel made of the point.

Do take a note of who has signed the letter. Appeal panels are independent of the admission authority, and must be seen to be so. There have been cases where Local Authority officials or clerks to the governing body signed letters. They should not. The only person who should be communicating with you about the result of your appeal is the clerk to the appeal. Anyone else, and it might suggest that the appeal was not independent of the admission authority.

The panel upholds your appeal

Congratulations. Everything you have worked for has come right, and the weeks, and perhaps months, of anguish were not in vain. The decision is binding on the admission authority so your child has a guaranteed place. You should then receive confirmation from the school very soon afterwards, and this will take you through the usual procedures for any new child joining the school. For you, the ordeal is over.

The panel does not uphold your appeal

Nationally, two out of three – and in some areas many more – parents who appeal will receive a letter telling them that their case was unsuccessful. This is a bitter blow and it may seem that all is lost. However, there are routes still left open to you.

You now need to make a decision: what is in the best interests of your child? Is it in your child's best interests to carry on, or would it be better to call it a day? If you decide to carry on, the following options are open to you.

Waiting lists

> *There is no statutory requirement for admission authorities to maintain waiting lists, and appeal panels have no power to determine where a child should be placed on the waiting list for a school. Panels should take no account of where the admission authority has placed a child on the waiting list, or of the fact that the parents of other children on the waiting list may not be appealing.*
> *School Admission Appeals Code of Practice, paragraph 4.76*

Admission authorities are not obliged to maintain waiting lists, although if they do maintain them there are rules covering how they are run. The most important thing is that they should not be run on a 'first come, first served' basis.

If you did not put your child's name on the list when you were denied a place, put it on now. The list should be prioritised according to the admission criteria, so your chances will depend on how well you match the criteria. Bear in mind that the list should be in order of priority, so your position is not fixed: anyone applying after you but having a higher priority will go higher up the list than you.

That being said, many children are admitted off the list, quite often at the very last minute. It is not uncommon for children to have been offered a place at a school only days before term is due to start.

Another appeal

The decision of the independent appeal panel is binding and the circumstances for making another direct appeal are limited. If you have appealed and were turned down, you may make another application in a later academic year. However, for many parents that is too long to wait, and would mean a year at one school before they could re-apply, with all the uncertainty that another application would bring.

> *Unless there are significant and material changes in the circumstances of the parent, child or school relevant to a further application, the admission authority may decide not to reach a fresh decision (or 'determination') in relation to such applications ... Where the admission authority has refused to consider another application for the same year group, no fresh appeal can be made. However, if its policy is not to consider repeat applications in the same academic year, unless there has been a change of circumstances relevant to the application, this policy must be clearly stated in the published admission arrangements.*
> **School Admission Appeals Code of Practice, paragraph 4.83**

Having made one appeal, you cannot apply again during the same academic year unless there are 'significant and material changes' to your application. Common examples of such changes in circumstances since the time at which the original application was made would be medical reasons, or that the family has moved house. It must be something that would cause the admission authority to reconsider their decision and change your priority according to the published admission criteria.

Admission authorities can refuse to reconsider your case if they don't feel that your circumstances have changed enough to warrant a fresh decision. This is not the same as refusing you a place (although the outcome is the same). If the admission authority refuses to reconsider your application then unfortunately there is little you can do. If, however, they do make a fresh decision and it still doesn't go your way, you can make another appeal and go through the whole appeal process all over again.

Other routes

There are three other routes you can go down, none of which have any guarantee of success, and all of which may incur additional cost. They will certainly incur additional stress.

It must be emphasised that all three routes are only open to you if you have reasonable grounds to think that the admission process and/or the appeal was not conducted properly. You cannot appeal simply because you don't like the answer.

Before undertaking any new course of action you should stop and consider very carefully if you want to go ahead. Is it really in the best interests of your child to prolong the decision? Is it in *your* interests? Is the allocated school so bad? Do take time to consider these points: it is very easy, in the days after being turned down by the panel, to make a decision in anger that may not, ultimately, be in your or your child's best interests.

Appeals to the Secretary of State for Education

The Secretary of State has limited powers with regard to appeals, and does not have the right to overturn the ruling of an appeal panel; nor does he or she have any review functions. The Secretary of State may only determine whether the appeal panel was correctly con-stituted and 'whether the admission authority or governing body has acted reasonably in exercising functions in respect of the appeal process'.

If, for example, the Secretary of State is satisfied that the Local Authority or governing body failed to constitute an appeal panel properly, he or she can direct them to appoint a properly constituted panel.

Very few appeals are made to the Secretary of State. Before embarking on such a course of action you should take advice from the local education authority – even if they are the admission authority against which you are appealing – or contact the Education Law Association.

Judicial review

The only body that can overturn the ruling of an independent appeal panel is a court. This is a very major step and one that may incur significant costs. It is not a step to be taken lightly.

A judicial review will not be successful simply because you didn't get the answer you were expecting. You must have reasonable grounds to lodge an appeal. Such grounds would include any suggestion that the process – either the admission process or the appeal – was so seriously flawed that a major injustice had occurred, or that some part of the process was in breach of other laws (such as discrimination or, more controversially, Human Rights legislation).

The grounds and scope of a judicial review lie far outside the remit of this book. If you wish to go down this path you should talk in the first instance to a solicitor, or to the Citizens Advice Bureau which may be able to put you in touch with lawyers with a history of dealing with educational cases.

Appeals to the Local Government Ombudsman

This is the most common, and easiest, route down which to go. About 1% of appeals (around about 1000 a year) go to the Local Government Ombudsman. Once again, do not think of the Ombudsman as some kind of court of final resort. Complaints to the Ombudsman are made when there is a suggestion that there was a fault in the way in which the proceedings were conducted – *not* because the panel reached a conclusion with which you don't agree.

It does seem that admission authorities other than Local Authorities (in other words, governing bodies of Foundation and VA schools) are more likely to be ruled against by the Ombudsman. This is not all that surprising, given the relative experience and resources of Local Authorities. But in the light of that very experience and resources, a worrying number of Local Authorities are still making mistakes that result in maladministration.

> *The Local Government Ombudsman can investigate written complaints about maladministration on the part of an admission appeal panel. This is not a right of appeal and has to relate to issues such as a failure to follow correct procedures or a failure to act independently and fairly, rather than just that the person making the complaint thinks that the decision is wrong.*
> *School Admission Appeals Code of Practice, paragraph 4.85*

The Ombudsman's powers are limited. Unlike the court, they cannot overturn a ruling, and they will only consider cases where there has been some suggestion of maladministration. And even if the Ombudsman finds that there was maladministration, it must be shown that your case suffered as a result of it. Just because an authority did not conduct its affairs properly does not mean that an injustice was done; it is perfectly possible that the right decision was reached even if the process was flawed.

Should the Ombudsman find that maladministration did occur and that your child was wrongfully denied a place, there are a number of possible solutions depending on when and how the mistake was made. If the admission process was carried out correctly but there were failings in the appeal, the most likely solution would be for the Ombudsman to ask for a fresh appeal hearing to be made.

In these circumstances the whole appeal process would be re-run, this time with a different panel and clerk. The new panel will have to consider the circumstances at the time of the second appeal, but also the fact that things may have changed at the school. It would be reasonable for the new panel to have some regard to the situation when the first appeal was made, particularly when considering factors such as the number of children on the school roll.

If, however, the Ombudsman found that the admission process was flawed and had unreasonably denied your child a place, the Ombudsman can ask the authority to admit your child. It will then be up to the admission authority whether or not to agree to the Ombudsman's ruling. Having had a ruling made against them by the Ombudsman, it would be unusual for an admission authority not to comply with the ruling. Ultimately, it would be up to the court to rule.

The Ombudsman can, and sometimes does, award compensation to parents who have been particularly ill served. Typically such awards are made when the parent or child has suffered unreasonable delays.

What constitutes maladministration?

Before considering an appeal to the Local Government Ombudsman, you would do well to get hold of a copy of the *Special Report on School Admissions and Appeals*. You can download a copy from the Ombudsman's website (http://www.lgo.org.uk) or order one free by telephoning 020 7217 4683. The Ombudsman also produces an annual report which is available on the website. Part of that report includes highlighted cases.

What is apparent from the reports is that maladministration can occur at almost every and any stage of the process. Because of this you should keep every document, every letter, and a note of every conversation you have with the admission authority. It may be the evidence you need to help convince the Ombudsman.

A lot of the areas that the Ombudsman covers have already been discussed in this book. Drawing from the Ombudsman's annual reports, the following extracts illustrate a wide range of the sorts of cases which have been considered maladministration. In all cases the appellant was either offered a fresh appeal, or their child was offered a place at the school.

Inappropriate participation

At the appeal hearing, one of the appeal committee members (the chairman of governors) was asked by the chair of the appeal committee to speak about the overcrowding difficulties faced by the school. The Ombudsman said that the roles of the governors' representative and governors who were members of the appeal committee should be kept completely separate. It was the responsibility of the governors' representative to put the case for the governing body. It was quite inappropriate for one of the governors who was on the appeal committee to speak on behalf of the governors or the school. That was maladministration.

No statement

The clerk to the appeal committee did not send the appellants a copy of the school's statement of the reasons for the decision to refuse the application (it appeared that the governors provided the committee with no such statement).

Briefings made without parents

The appellants were not present when the appeal committee was briefed by the clerk before the hearing began about the school's admission policy, the criteria for admission, the number of applications received, the number of places offered, the area from which children had been offered places on grounds of proximity, and the problems caused by the shortage of school places in the borough.

One governors' representative took refreshment and lunch breaks with the appeal committee in the absence of any appellants.

Failing to do their job properly

The written statement provided by the governors merely asserted that places were offered in accordance with the published criteria, and that once the places had been filled, up to the standard number, any further admissions would prejudice the efficient and effective provision of education and the use of resources for other students.

The appeal committee was required to satisfy itself at what point prejudice would arise and what the degree of prejudice would be if the appellants' child were admitted. It was not sufficient for an appeal committee simply to accept the governors' assertions about this; the committee had to be seen to form its own view, having given the appellants the opportunity to make any representations on the subject. The committee's decision had to be explicit, not implicit, and it should have been expressly recorded. The Ombudsman found that the committee did not properly satisfy itself at what point prejudice would arise or properly record its decision.

Not carrying out the balancing stage

The Code of Practice makes it clear that an appeal committee must take into account not only the school's admission arrangements, but also the case put forward by the parent. Parents were not restricted to making arguments solely about the school's criteria, and the appeal committee had to make an independent judgement on the basis of all the arguments put forward, not just the admission criteria.

Not listening to the evidence provided

Ms A explained that her child had serious disabilities, such that she had a good case for admission under the medical criterion. The appeal committee did not give adequate consideration to this point on the grounds that Ms A had not mentioned it on the original application form. The published admission arrangement stated that medical factors had to be mentioned at the time of application – or if not, by the time the date for decisions to be taken on admissions was reached – and that medical factors would otherwise not be taken into account. Naturally, the governors in making admission decisions could only take account of the information they were given on the application form. But this was not a point which should have fettered the decision of the appeal committee, which was required to take account of all the evidence put before it. At the appeal Ms A fully explained the medical point. It was wrong for the appeal committee to dismiss it solely on the grounds that she did not mention it on the original application form.

Judging the appellant, not the case

Mrs A had questioned the Headteacher's absence from the appeal hearings. Two committee members and the clerk said that Mrs A had been aggressive and the clerk believed that the low rating of her appeal given by the members was a result of her aggressive manner. The Ombudsman said this was irrelevant, and commented: 'Statutory appeals must be determined solely on relevant grounds: an appellant's demeanour at the hearing is not, in my view, relevant to the task of the decision-takers.'

Measuring at fault
When the council told Mrs T that it was unable to offer her daughter a place at the school, it gave her no information about the key distances. That information was not provided in the written case made by the council for the appeal. At the appeal hearing there was no map available to show the location of those children who had been offered places on geographical grounds. The council's presenting officer gave information to the hearing about the distance from home to school for her daughter, and for the last child to be accepted under the geographical criterion. But that information was subsequently shown to be incorrect.

Same person appearing twice
One member of the appeal committee was unable to attend the appeal. The school filled the vacancy with a governor who normally acted at appeals as presenting officer for the school's case. The governor who filled the vacancy said that, although no-one appeared at the hearing of Mr G's appeal formally on behalf of the governors to put the school's case, she herself covered the ground of her normal presentation. In effect, she was wearing two hats. The Ombudsman found this extraordinary and commented: 'Given her normal role I doubt she could ever be seen as a proper choice, and her actions cast doubt on the fairness of the entire proceedings.'

Failing to prove prejudice
The Ombudsman was not satisfied that the panel considered properly the question of prejudice. The school's case to the panel made no mention of difficulties which would arise if more children were to be admitted to the school. The school simply restated its admission number and that it would be detrimental to the education of all the students to admit more children. The Ombudsman pointed out that this was contrary to the Code of Practice and was maladministration. The panel had little evidence on which to base any decision about whether prejudice would be caused by additional admissions.

Rush job
The programme for the appeal hearing set aside ten minutes for each case. The panel members all said that the time was adequate and, if hearings over-ran, that they were able to catch up later. But the Ombudsman commented: 'The timescale set down was likely to generate the perception that the appeal hearing was no more than a

token exercise, bearing in mind that time should be allowed for the school's case to be fully presented and questioned as well as the parents' case.'

Adding extra criteria
The second reason given for refusing the application was that Mrs A had not given the school as her first preference. But the admission criteria made no provision for the governors to take account of whether the school was or was not a first preference.

Withholding information
No information was provided to Ms M about how to appeal or how the appeal process worked. She was not aware that she could take someone with her to support her during the appeal. Had she known that, she would have made such an arrangement.

Made their mind up before the meeting
One panel member said that the panel knew from the start, before any appeals were heard, that the school was full. He pointed out that it was a well-known fact that the school was oversubscribed each year – a fact that was published in the local press. The Ombudsman pointed out that natural justice required the decision of the panel to be based on the evidence presented, including evidence presented by parents who were appealing. The decision could not be either wholly or partly based on the local knowledge or opinions of the panel members.

One nightmare appeal
The Ombudsman found no fewer than 15 faults in the admission and appeal arrangements. Amongst those faults were the following:

- Before the appeal hearings, the appeal panel consulted the governors about the number of appeals which might be allowed, but the appellants were not involved in that discussion.
- The governors provided no evidence to support their assertion that they had correctly applied their admission criteria, and the panel did not test that assertion.
- The governors' statement in advance did not attempt to demonstrate prejudice to education in the school if more pupils were admitted, so appellants had no notice of the case to be made.
- At times, the panel operated with only two of the three members present – but the third member nonetheless took part in decisions about appeals where she had not heard the evidence.

How to appeal to the Ombudsman

There are three Local Government Ombudsmen in England. Each of them deals with complaints from different parts of the country:

London boroughs north of the river Thames (including Richmond, but not including Harrow), Essex, Kent, Surrey, Suffolk, East and West Sussex, Berkshire, Buckinghamshire, Hertfordshire and the City of Coventry:

Local Government Ombudsman
21 Queen Anne's Gate
London SW1H 9BU
Tel: 020 7915 3210
Fax: 020 7233 0396

City of Birmingham, Cheshire, Derbyshire, Nottinghamshire, Lincolnshire and the north of England (except the Cities of York and Lancaster):

Local Government Ombudsman
Beverley House
17 Shipton Road
York YO30 5FZ
Tel: 01904 663200
Fax: 01904 663269

London boroughs south of the river Thames (except Richmond) and Harrow; the Cities of York and Lancaster; and the rest of England, not included in the other two offices' areas:

Local Government Ombudsman
The Oaks
No. 2 Westwood Way
Westwood Business Park
Coventry CV4 8JB
Tel: 024 7669 5999
Fax: 024 7669 5902

To register a complaint, contact the relevant office as soon as you know the outcome of your appeal. You should promptly assemble any evidence that you have of maladministration, as the Ombudsman tends to move relatively quickly once an appeal has been lodged.

You will need to provide the Ombudsman with any evidence you have to support your claim of maladministration.

CHAPTER 8

Special cases

Infant class size prejudice. When can an admission authority claim infant class size prejudice? How the appeal process is conducted for infant class size prejudice. Multiple appeals. Appeals to schools of a selective nature and to sixth forms. Parents of twice-excluded children/Pupils with challenging behaviour

Infant class size prejudice

Appeals to infant classes, the first years at primary school, may fall into a different category of appeal due to laws that set a maximum size of class. Infant classes – which comprise the foundation class (formerly known as reception), Year 1 and Year 2 – cannot by law be larger than 30 children without the school taking 'qualifying measures', typically employing an extra teacher.

The effect of this on appeals is quite profound. If you are applying to a primary school then you may run into the special case of infant class size prejudice. This limits the scope of the appeal and reduces your chances of success. Effectively, what the limit on class sizes says is that a class of more than 30 is by definition prejudicial to efficient education and the efficient use of resources.

If the panel concludes that infant class size prejudice will occur then there is no balancing stage to the appeal.

This is a much tougher call. There is no discretion by the panel to consider if the school can take children over the published admission number; nor does the panel have any grounds on which to consider the individual circumstances of the parents and/or child and balance them against the prejudice the school will suffer. Infant class size prejudice appeals are almost certainly the toughest appeals to win. For this reason it would work very much in your favour if you could successfully challenge the grounds for infant class size prejudice and just fight an ordinary prejudice appeal.

Not every appeal to an infant class would fall under infant class size prejudice. If the school to which you are appealing has classes of

> Infant classes of 5, 6 and 7 year olds may not contain more than 30 pupils with a single qualified teacher. Admission authorities may not refuse admission to an infant class on 'prejudice' grounds (for class-size-related reasons) unless the number of applications for places at the school exceeds the published admission number, and measures to keep to the statutory class-size limit would result in prejudice to efficient education or the efficient use of resources.
>
> School Admissions Code of Practice, paragraph 7.18

fewer than 30, and even if your child were to be admitted the class size would still be under 30, then it is not a case of infant class size prejudice and falls under the normal rules.

When you receive the case from the admission authority it should be clear whether they are claiming infant class size prejudice. If you are in any doubt, call the admission authority and check. Because of the limited grounds on which you can win an infant class size prejudice appeal, you need to plan how to tackle the case. As we have already seen, however, you should not limit yourself to preparing only an infant class size appeal. There may be grounds on which to dispute infant class size prejudice, which if successful would mean that it would be a normal appeal.

Because of the nature of infant admissions, admission authorities with two or three intakes a year into foundation should consider all applications for admission of 'rising fives' at the same time. This enables them to have regard to class-size legislation while not disadvantaging parents who may want, or have, to defer their child's entry to the school until later in the academic year. It also ensures that all appeals can be heard at the same time, regardless of the term in which the pupil is to enter the school. If parents defer entry of their child to later in the academic year, a panel should regard their place in the same way as if the child had already taken it up.

When can an admission authority claim infant class size prejudice?

A few rather obvious points. First, it must be an infant class: admission authorities cannot claim class size prejudice for junior admissions (i.e. admissions into Yr 3 and above). Also, they can only claim prejudice where to admit a child would take the class over 30 children.

Some other cases seem simple enough, but are in fact not quite what they appear. The Local Government Ombudsman reported one case where the admission authority claimed infant class size prejudice for a school with an admission number of 55. The classes were arranged into one class of 30 and one of 25. The authority claimed that because of space limitations, no more children could be admitted to the class of 25, and could only be admitted to the class of 30. They therefore claimed that all appeals were infant class size prejudice.

The Ombudsman found that this was not the case. The limitation to put extra children only into the class of 30 was one the authority had made; a child did not necessarily have to go into that class, and therefore it was not a case of infant class size prejudice. The admission authority may have had good grounds for an appeal on ordinary prejudice, but the appeal panel would then be able to go to the balancing stage of the appeal and the parent's case would be heard.

Admission authorities must also take into account the effect on admissions as children move up the school from foundation into Years 1 and 2, where the same class-size restrictions apply. If the school can show that because of the way it organises its year groups, admitting too many children into foundation will result in classes of more than 30 in either Year 1 or Year 2, requiring it to take qualifying measures, then that is infant class size prejudice.

> **CASE STUDY**
> Ms P appealed against a decision not to admit her son to a Local Authority primary. The published admission number was 45, with two foundation classes of 21 and 24. The Local Authority claimed infant class size prejudice; the appeal panel agreed. The school had five classes in its infant school – two foundation classes, one Yr 1 class of 30, one joint Yr1/Yr2 class of 30 and one Yr 2 class of 30. To admit Ms P's son would require the school to take qualifying measures in subsequent years. The panel did not uphold Ms P's claim.

There are some exceptions to the rules, and these are known as 'excepted pupils'. Essentially, if you apply outside the normal admission round (see also pp. 23–4) and your child is admitted under very specific criteria (see overleaf), then the school is permitted to have class sizes over 30, but only for the remainder of that school year. For the next school year, if the cohort remained the same size, then the school would have to arrange its classes so that they were smaller than 30, or take qualifying measures to deal with it.

> The class size legislation makes sensible allowance for the entry of an additional child in certain limited circumstances where not to admit the child would be prejudicial to his or her interests ('excepted pupils'). These circumstances include:
>
> - where a child moves into an area outside the normal admission round and there is no other school which would provide suitable education within a reasonable distance of his or her home;
> - where the child receives a statement of special educational needs naming the school, or a pupil with a statement naming that school moves into the area, in each case outside the normal admission round;
> - where a pupil is initially refused admission to a school but is subsequently offered a place there for one of two reasons: the person making the original decision recognises that an error was made in implementing the school's admission arrangements; or an admission appeal panel upholds an appeal;
> - in addition, to preserve the important benefits for children with special educational needs which may be derived from attending mainstream classes, a child normally educated in a special educational needs unit attached to a mainstream school or in a special school will be treated as an excepted pupil for any time when he or she is in an infant class in the mainstream school.
>
> In the first three of these cases, the class may only be above 30 for the remainder of that school year.
> *School Admissions Code of Practice, paragraph A.44*

How the appeal process is conducted for infant class size prejudice

The appeal takes a similar form to an ordinary appeal, and all the regulations and timescales are exactly the same . However, the panel has different considerations and must conduct the appeal in a slightly different way.

The panel must make several judgements. First, it must decide whether the admission authority has made its case for infant class size prejudice. Just because the admission authority claims that infant class size prejudice will occur, does not make it so: the panel must make up its own mind.

If, in the panel's view, no case is made, then the appeal becomes an ordinary prejudice appeal and the panel can move onto considering the second, balancing stage.

If, however, they do find that it is a question of infant class size prejudice then the panel's options become limited. The panel can only allow your appeal if it is satisfied:

- that the decision to refuse admission was not one which a reasonable admission authority would make in the circumstances of the case (this is known in the Code of Practice as 'Ground A'); or
- that the child would have been offered a place if the admission arrangements had been properly implemented ('Ground B').

Ground B
Looking first at Ground B, this is broadly speaking similar to the instruction to panels under normal hearings to see if the admission criteria were correctly applied. Ground B does leave you some room to manoeuvre. For example, if the admission criteria were based on distance to school, and you were able to show that a child who lived further away was awarded a place while you were not, then that would be a case to uphold the appeal under Ground B. This is a technical ruling based solely on the admission authority's ability to carry out its job properly. As we have seen in Chapter 1, there are problem areas for admission authorities, particularly when it comes to tests of religious faith (see pp. 15–17).

CASE STUDY
Mr L and Ms J appealed against a decision not to admit Ms J's child to a VA primary. The published admission number was 30. The school claimed infant class size prejudice. Mr L had a son at the school, but the admission authority claimed that this did not constitute a sibling under their definition. The panel rejected the school's case. As evidence they cited the Local Authority definition which included half-siblings and step-siblings under the rule. They considered that a reasonable authority would have admitted the child, so upheld the appeal.

The Code of Practice does rather limit your ability to sway the panel. Paragraph 4.57 says that the panel can only look at new evidence if this evidence helps to highlight the existing error: in other words, the panel can't look at new factors that were not available to the admission authority. For example, if a parent failed to mention on their application that their child had a compelling medical reason, and the admission authority gave priority to such cases, the appeal panel could not take this into account as the admission authority did not know that – nor could it reasonably be expected to know that. If, however, a parent had drawn attention to the child's medical condition but the authority had ruled against it because they did not fully appreciate the seriousness of the condition, then as a parent you could introduce new evidence to back up your case – such as a letter from a consultant. In these circumstances the panel would be correct in accepting that new evidence because it assisted in identifying the original error.

Other examples could include failing to give regard to a sibling, or in faith schools, not accepting (or misunderstanding) the letter from the minister.

Because Ground B is the equivalent of a 'get out of jail free' card, you should study very carefully the way in which the admission authority conducted the admission process. Is there anything that they did which could give you grounds to appeal under Ground B?

> *In considering an appeal under Ground B, the panel should only consider the material available to the admission authority when it made its decision, together with material that the authority would have been aware of if it had acted reasonably, although the panel may allow fresh material such as a letter or a statement to be submitted by the parents in order to assist in identifying the original error.*
> *School Admission Appeals Code of Practice, paragraph 4.57*

One further point is that in order for a Ground B appeal to be successful, you must show not only that the admission authority failed to do its job properly, but also that *because* it failed to do its job properly, your child was denied a place. Say, for example, the admission authority used distance as a tie-breaker but measured the distance to your house incorrectly. The error is only relevant to the appeal if you can show that had the authority measured the distance properly, your child would have got in. They may have made the right decision, but based it on the wrong evidence. What is under scrutiny here is the decision, not how it was reached.

Ground A

Ground A appeals appear to offer slightly more hope, but are in fact very tightly reined-in by the word 'reasonable'. Tests of reasonableness are notoriously difficult, but there is legal precedent that provides some guidance. What was seemingly an obscure 1948 ruling has become the lodestone for such tests. Essentially, a reasonable decision is one that any sensible authority would have made, in this case taking into account the admission authority's policy and the organisation of the school.

When it comes to Ground A, the appeal panel has slightly more leeway in terms of what it can consider. As we saw, Ground B can only take into consideration the information that a panel could reasonably be expected to have had at the time it made the decision. Ground A is slightly wider in scope, and can consider fresh evidence. However, the High Court has ruled that any evidence that is admitted would have to be persuasive.

Ground A is not an easy call. In order to win a Ground A call you need to show not that the admission authority carried out its procedures incorrectly, but that its ruling was unreasonable – in other words, that what it did was perverse.

In considering the reasonableness of the admission authority's decision, the panel must determine whether it would be perverse to refuse to admit the particular child. It should take into consideration: the reasons for the published admission arrangements and the parent's preference; the circumstances of the particular child and family; and the practical consequences for both the school and other children competing for places in the relevant infant class or classes if the child were to be admitted. However, the appeal panel has no power to analyse whether the admission arrangements themselves are reasonable or perverse.

School Admission Appeals Code of Practice, paragraph 4.59

How this helps you
If you suspect that you are facing an infant class size appeal, you should prepare your case very well. The authority should indicate in their first letter if they consider it a case of infant class size prejudice. If they don't, and the published admission number is near to 30 (anything from 27 up), then assume it is and prepare two cases – one supposing infant class size prejudice, and another, ordinary prejudice.

However, even if you are told it is a case of infant class size prejudice, you should prepare a case with a balancing stage. The panel may not accept the admission authority's claim that it is infant class size prejudice, in which case a normal appeal will be heard.

You probably stand a better chance of success with an appeal based on Ground B – that the admission authority did not apply the admission criteria properly, and that because of this, your child was unfairly denied a place. Ground A seems to be slightly easier, but in fact the very close definition of reasonableness means that the scope is limited.

Multiple or group appeals

Most appeals to popular schools following the normal admission round will be multiple appeals. This presents the appeal panel with an additional task. Unless there are only very few parents appealing, it is unlikely that the panel will be able to admit all the children without prejudice to efficient education and the efficient use of resources taking place. So the panel, as well as deciding its usual tasks, must also decide at what point prejudice occurs. It may decide that the admission authority's case is proved and that admitting even one extra child will cause prejudice. But it may feel that the authority's case is not proved and, for whatever reasons, may decide that a number of children could be admitted before prejudice occurs. The panel will admit up to that number and then decide beyond that on the individual cases as to whether the needs of the parent and/or child outweigh the problems the school will suffer if they admit the child.

In deciding which children to admit, the panel may have some regard to the admission criteria, but also to other factors in the individual parents' cases so that any compelling reasons for admission which the parent presents can be taken into account.

First, the panel should assess whether admitting all the pupils would cause prejudice to efficient education or the efficient use of resources ('prejudice'), and whether the child would have been offered a place if the admission arrangements had been properly implemented. If the panel finds that admission of the appellants would not cause such prejudice, then their appeals should be upheld. Second, if the panel decides that admission of additional children would result in prejudice, it should consider, for each individual case, whether the parent's grounds for their child to be admitted to the school outweigh such prejudice. This involves no comparison between appellants' cases. However, if there are several cases which outweigh the prejudice to the school and merit admission, but the panel determines that the school could not cope with that number of successful appeals, the panel should then compare cases and decide which of them to uphold.

School Admission Appeals Code of Practice, paragraph 4.71

No decisions as to which children are to be admitted can be made until every appeal has been heard. Only then will the panel have the right information on which to make its judgement.

Where an admission authority is faced with a large number of appeals (for popular schools it is not uncommon for a panel to sit for three to five days), it makes sense to group them and deal with them in as quick a way as possible. The law permits admission authorities to conduct these appeals in a different way, although there is no requirement for them to do so; many prefer simply to run dozens of individual appeals.

However, if an authority decides to run group appeals, the process is slightly different. The appeal has two quite separate parts: the first is a group hearing to which every parent who has lodged an appeal is invited to attend; the second is the individual hearing, which may take place on a different day.

At the group hearing, which takes place in front of the appeal panel, the admission authority lays out its general case. It will explain how the admission criteria are applied, and why it believes prejudice will occur if one more child is admitted. The presenting officer will then be cross-questioned not only by the panel, but also by any parent present at the hearing. Once everyone who wishes to speak has raised their questions and points, the meeting is over and the panel will consider if the authority has made a case for prejudice. If no case has been made, then all the appeals must be allowed and nothing more needs to be done.

It is more likely, though, that either the case for prejudice is proved and no more children can be admitted, or the panel feels that a certain number of additional children can be admitted. Whichever of these occurs, the panel will then move to the second stage of the appeal and hear each case individually without the other parents present.

As the panel will have already considered the question of prejudice, the individual appeals will be to determine whether the admission criteria were applied correctly to each individual child, and if not, whether the child was unfairly denied a place. If you are in that position, and can prove that your child would have been offered a place had the admission authority not made the mistake, then your appeal must be upheld. This does not affect any other appeals. To make that clear, if the panel decides it can admit five children before prejudice occurs, but you can show that your child was unfairly denied a place, your child will be admitted in addition to the five others, not as one of them. This is true even for infant class size prejudice appeals (this would come under Ground B).

The other function of the individual appeals is to conduct the balancing stage – the weighing-up of the competing needs of school and parent. This is the same process as would be followed in an ordinary appeal.

During the individual hearings, the admission authority cannot introduce any new evidence at all unless it comes up in questioning.

It would be unfair for the authority to start bringing in new evidence as the individual appeals go on, as that would mean that earlier parents would not have had the chance to comment on or consider it. If, however, new evidence comes out in the questioning of the admission authority's evidence, the clerk will have to ensure that the appeal panel considers what bearing the evidence may have on all the appeals, and should decide how best to advise so that the panel deals with the matter fairly. This may entail adjourning the appeals to give other parents the opportunity to consider and challenge the new evidence.

Only when all the appeals have been heard may the panel sit to consider the cases. That being said, it is common practice for panels to sit at the end of each day to review the cases they have heard that day and to begin a filtering process to rank those appeals that stand little chance of success apart from those that merit further consideration.

How this helps you
Whether your authority holds group appeals or individual ones, it should make little difference to how you prepare your case. However, you may wish to consider how to approach the group hearing. You need to consider how to reveal the information you have. Do you want to share it with other parents so that they can use the argument in their own cases, or do you want to keep it for your own private individual hearing?

Say, for example, you discover that the admission authority has made a mistake in its admission process regarding distance measurements. You need to consider how you reveal that information. In the interests of natural justice you could show to all the parents at the meeting that a mistake was made. Every parent would therefore benefit from your discovery. The effect of that could be that the admission authority reviews all the cases, and other children are admitted but not your child. You did the right thing, but has it got your child a place? As a parent who wants to get your child into the school, have you done the right thing by him or her?

Might it be better *not* to reveal this key finding of yours at the public meeting, but to use it instead at your individual hearing? In theory it should make not a jot of difference: the appeal panel should reconsider every appeal to see if the same mistake was made with regard to other applications – and you might end up in the same position as if you had made your finding public at the hearing.

Realistically, though, that is unlikely. Panels are under a lot of pressure, and are very busy. Chances are that if your case is well put, the panel will accept the finding in your case but not apply it retrospectively to every other case. That sounds very cynical indeed – and to be honest, it is. But it is realistic.

What to ask at the public meeting

Use the meeting to find out as much as you can about how the admission authority conducted its business. If the presenting officer does not make it clear, ask him or her to explain exactly how the criteria were applied. Use the time to fill in any information gaps that you may have about the process. This is particularly important if you are applying to an infant class and the authority is claiming infant class size prejudice.

Listen out for anything that might suggest some kind of inter-pretation of the admission criteria. It is unlikely that anyone is going to say 'what we mean by this is not quite how it is written' – that would be an open season for appeals – but presenting officers will often reveal that perhaps the criteria were open to some interpretation. This is more likely to be the case with schools of a religious nature which have some kind of subjective test, rather than other schools which may have simple sibling and/or distance rules.

Appeals to schools of a selective nature, and to sixth forms

Selective schools (grammar schools) are one of only two categories of maintained school that are allowed to keep places empty if they do not have enough children of the required standard. (The other, although not strictly relevant, is state boarding schools which do not have to admit day pupils if there are unfilled boarding places.)

There are a few 'bilateral schools' that maintain both a selective stream and a non-selective stream. Bilateral schools may not keep selective places empty if they do not have enough children to fill them.

Some specialist schools reserve up to 10% of their intake for pupils showing an aptitude for the specialism. These schools must make it clear how they will measure that aptitude, and whatever system they use must be in accordance with the principles of admission policies (clearly defined and objectively assessable). But unlike fully selective schools, specialist schools may not keep unfilled places empty. If they are unable to fill the 10% of places with suitable children they must offer those places to children who fall into other admission categories.

Grammar schools have a number of ways of assessing suitability for children to be admitted, although all will have some kind of academic test to determine the academic abilities of the children applying. Sixth forms will usually use GCSE results to determine their admissions.

> *The panel's role, as for appeals to other schools, is to consider an appeal against the decision to refuse admission and to determine whether the child should be admitted to the school. The panel should not attempt to make its own assessment of a child's ability, but may need to decide whether the original decision that the child was not of the required standard was reasonable.*
> *School Admission Appeals Code of Practice, paragraph 4.65*

Some authorities for grammar schools also have a review system to consider whether children who don't quite make the grade should be admitted. This does not have any effect on your right to appeal, and the fact that your child has been through the review should not affect your chances at appeal.

The role of the appeal panel is largely the same as for any other appeal. The process is identical and the job of the panel is the same. Were the rules correctly applied; will prejudice occur if your child is admitted; is there a balance to be struck?

You should be aware that it is not the panel's role to make its own assessment of your child's ability. Its role is to review whether the process to determine your child's ability was fair under the circumstances. Getting your child to re-sit the exam is not likely to sway a panel.

In addition to the normal appeals case, if your child failed to make the required grade but you still wish to apply, you will need to have a case to explain why they did not do as well as predicted. Typical extenuating circumstances for your child not making the grade could include:

- medical reasons – e.g. illness leading up to or during the tests, suppported by evidence as to why this would have an impact on your child's result.
- family circumstances – e.g. separation, divorce or death of a family member on the day of the test, or so recently as to have had a likely impact on the test.
- social – e.g. where English is not the main language of the family, and no provision is made by the examination authority to allow for this.

Another area the panel must consider is whether your child was subjected to discrimination if they have particular special needs or a medical condition. For example, if a child who sits the test is dyslexic, you could claim discrimination if no provision is made for that, as the child would have been treated less favourably than a child without the condition. However, had the school made allowance for the child by granting extra time to take the test, or by giving them a reader, that would constitute a reasonable adjustment to the test and would not be discriminatory under the terms of the DDA.

Equally well, it would be expected for a child suffering from hearing loss to be seated near to the front of the hall so that he or she could lip-read as the examiner talked – or alternatively, for them to be allowed to take the test in a room with low ambient noise.

As long as the admission authority has made 'reasonable' allowance for a child's disability, disability on its own is unlikely to be grounds for an appeal.

Some parents have tried, and failed, to claim that selective tests are by their nature discriminatory and should be illegal. This claim has never been upheld. The Disability Rights Commission recognises the legality of selective testing.

If you apply to a selective school outside the normal admission round, the school may not offer a facility to test your child. In that situation, if the admission authority is not willing to accept that such a casual applicant is of the required academic ability for admission, it must make arrangements for an appropriate assessment of the child's ability to be made if their parent lodges an appeal. If this is not done, the panel must work on the assumption that the child is of the required academic standard, and should follow the normal two-stage process of any appeal.

Parents of twice-excluded children/Pupils with challenging behaviour

Where a child has been permanently excluded from two or more schools, and at least one of the exclusions took place after 1 September 1997, parents can still express a preference for a school place. However, the admission authority does not have to comply with your wishes for a period of two years following the second or any subsequent expulsion. There are some exceptions to this: children who were below compulsory school age when excluded; pupils who were reinstated following a permanent exclusion; and pupils who would have been reinstated following a permanent exclusion had it been practicable to do so.

If your child falls into this category, your right to an appeal to an independent appeal panel is lost. There is an appeal process, but this is for the school to appeal against a decision by the Local Authority to require the school to admit the child.

> *Admission authorities for certain schools, or Academies, may decide to refuse to admit a challenging child where there are places available, on the grounds that admission would prejudice the provision of efficient education or the efficient use of resources. This will normally only be appropriate where a school has a particularly high concentration of pupils with challenging behaviour, or the child is particularly challenging, and in either case the school:*
>
> a. *is under special measures or has recently come out of them (within the last two years); or*
> b. *has been identified by OFSTED as having serious weaknesses; or*
> c *is subject to a formal warning notice; or*
> d. *is a Fresh Start school or Academy open for less than two years; or*
> e. *is a secondary school where less than 25% of whose pupils are achieving five or more GCSEs at grades A*–C.*
>
> *School Admissions Code of Practice, paragraph 7.7*

There is no parental representation at this appeal; it is between the Local Authority and the school's governing body. However, the parents should be informed as soon as the decision has been made.

Parental choice can also be limited under other circumstances. If you apply outside the normal admission round, under exceptional circumstances an admission authority may refuse to admit your child if they have challenging behaviour. As a parent you would then be entitled to an appeal in front of an independent appeal panel. This is a normal prejudice appeal. The admission authority's case will be that to admit your child will, by the challenging behaviour that your child exhibits, prejudice the efficient education and efficient use of resources at the school.

If you are in such a position, your appeal will be based on the same principles as any other appeal, but in addition you will need to challenge the authority's case that your child's behaviour is disruptive and likely to cause these problems. It is unlikely that any admission authority would use these powers without some very firm evidence backed up by medical opinion. In turn you would need to show how that was in the past, and that by effective management such problems would not re-occur.

Given the nature of the schools that can use these powers, and the exceptional circumstances when they may be used, refusing entrance to pupils with challenging behaviour is not a common occurrence.

Appendix 1

Proposed changes to the codes for admissions and admission appeals, brought in by the Education Act 2006

The revised codes for admissions and admission appeals are likely to come into effect in February 2007 for use in the 2007–2008 admission round. The changes are significant and are likely to have an effect on parental choice and on your likelihood of success at appeal.

One of the most significant changes to both codes is an alteration in their legal status. Under the existing law, admission authorities were legally bound to 'have regard' for the codes. A successful challenge in the High Court meant that as long as the authority could demonstrate regard for the codes in its deliberations, it was not bound to follow their provisions. This loophole has now been closed: the new codes are statutory and admission authorities must follow them explicitly.

The most significant changes under review are to the School Admissions Code of Practice, and are as follows.

Interviewing of parents:

Section 88A of the School Standards and Framework Act 1998 (as inserted by the Education and Inspections Act 2006) prohibits the interviewing of parents and/or children as method for deciding whether a child should be offered a place at a school. This includes both face-to-face interviews and those using the telephone or other means, for example written questions and answers and essays. Open days and other events for prospective parents and children are not affected.

> *Staff and governors are encouraged to meet parents at open evenings and on other occasions, but information gained in this way must not play a part in the admission decision-making process. Attendance at an open evening or other meeting at the school must not be a condition for the allocation of a place.*

Additional information:

> *Admission authorities must not use supplementary application or information forms that ask:*
>
> *a) for personal details about parents, such as criminal convictions or marital, occupational or financial status;*
> *b) for details about parents' achievement, educational background or whether their first language is English;*
> *c) for details about parents' or children's disabilities, special educational needs or medical conditions unless this is in support of positive action;*
> *d) about parents' or children's interests, hobbies or membership of societies.*
>
> *Admission authorities must not discriminate against children whose parents fall into certain social groups. No personal information about parents is relevant in considering an application for a place at a school, and criteria which focus on parents cannot legitimately be included in oversubscription criteria.*
>
> *At schools designated as having a religious character, [the above] prohibitions do not prevent the use of a supplementary form that asks parents or children about their membership of or relationship with the church or religious denomination.*

Changes to permitted oversubscription criteria:

> *In setting oversubscription criteria, admission authorities must not:*
>
> *a) stipulate conditions that change the priority given to an application;*
> *b) give priority to children according to the order of other schools named as preferences by their parents, including 'first preference first' arrangements, subject [to certain conditions];*
> *c) give higher priority to children whose parents are more able or willing to support the ethos of the school or to support the school financially or in some other way;*

d) *give higher priority to children according to the occupational or financial status of parents;*

e) *give higher priority to children according to the educational or social group or background of their parents;*

f) *take account of reports from primary or nursery schools about past behaviour, attitude or achievement;*

g) *discriminate against or disadvantage children with special educational needs or disabilities;*

h) *allocate places at a school on the basis that a sibling or other relative is a former pupil;*

i) *take account of the behaviour of other members of a child's family, whether good or bad, including a good or bad attendance record;*

j) *take account of parents' marital status;*

k) *give priority to children whose parents are current or former staff or governors or who have another connection to the school;*

l) *give priority to children who (or whose parents) have particular interests, specialist knowledge or hobbies;*

m) *give priority to children based on the order in which applications were received;*

n) *in the case of grammar schools, give priority to siblings of current pupils;*

o) *expressly exclude applicants from a particular social or religious group, or state that only applicants from a particular social or religious group will be considered for admission.*

Appendix 2

Suggested sizes for secondary school teaching areas

The following figures are taken from the government advice on buildings for new secondary schools. It shows the recommended areas for each type of room according to the different category.

Space type	Recommended area (m^2) according to group size		
	20	25	30
small classroom	35	43	51
standard classroom/seminar room	43	51	60
large classroom	48	57	66
ICT room or business studies	55	66	77
language laboratory	55	66	77
science laboratory KS3/4		77	90
sixth form science laboratory	77	90	
general art room for KS3/4		77	90
large art room (textiles or 3D)		90	105
sixth form art room	77	90	

Space type	Recommended area (m²) according to group size		
	20	25	30
dry textiles room	90		
graphics room	77		
graphics/product	90		
electronics and control systems	90		
resistant materials	112		
resistant materials/engineering	116		
food room	101		
music classroom		57	67
music recital room		77	90
drama/audio-visual studio		77	90

Source: Building Bulletin 98: Briefing Framework for Secondary School Projects

In primary schools the calculation is rather simpler. A classbase to support a class of 30 children should be no smaller than 49m² with a further ancillary space of 14m².

There are further calculations concerning halls, toilets, common spaces, corridors, etc. For more information on these and other guidelines, see *Assessing the Net Capacity of Schools* (DfES/0739/2001 REV) obtainable from www.dfes.gov.uk, or email dfes@prolog.uk.com.

For very detailed guidance see *Building Bulletin 98* available from the DfES.

Appendix 3

Sample letters

Letter giving notice of appeal

Mr Simon Chair
Chairman of Governors
Blankshire High School
Anytown
Blankshire BL1 1BL

Dear Mr Chair

**Letter of admissions appeal on behalf of Joe Smith
(d.o.b. 30 Sep 94)**

We have recently received a letter of rejection for our application for a place in September 20XX at your school for our son, Joe. This has obviously come as a bitter disappointment both to ourselves and, more importantly, to Joe. Whilst we realise that there are a limited number of places at your school, we wish to appeal on behalf of Joe for a place.

We look forward hopefully to hearing from you.

Yours sincerely

Letter submitting appeal

Mrs Barbara Clerk
Clerk to the Appeal Panel
Blankshire High School
Anytown
Blankshire BL1 1BL

Dear Mrs Clerk

Appeal on behalf of Joe Smith (d.o.b. 30 Sep 94)

Please find enclosed the written statement we would wish the panel to consider for our appeal against the governing body's decision not to offer our son Joe a place at Blankshire High School in September 20XX.

The appeal comprises a three-page statement accompanied by two letters of recommendation; one from his current Headteacher, Mrs A Headteacher, and a letter from his football coach, Mr M Football.

Should we wish to add other information to our appeal, we will endeavour to do so before the appeal hearing. It may well be that when we see the written statement from the school, we will wish to add something.

Yours sincerely

Sample appeal case

This fictional case is an appeal for the balancing stage of the appeal. The case is not a strong one, relying mainly on the fact that Joe is to be separated from his current friends, and there is a suggestion of bullying. The parents have painted a good pen picture of their son. At the hearing they would need to develop some of the themes here (see the relevant chapters of the book).

Appeal for admission to Blankshire High School For *Joe Smith*, d.o.b. 30 Sep 94

We are writing to appeal against the decision not to give our child Joe a place at Blankshire School.

We feel that an education at Blankshire High School will be best for Joe's education and welfare. In particular we believe:

- The ethos and values of the school are such as to provide the right environment for Joe to prosper.
- That if Joe attends his allocated school he will be subjected to continued bullying.

The ethos and values of the school are such as to provide the right environment for Joe to prosper.

About Joe

Joe is an above-average boy who has done well in his time at Little Snoring Primary School. He achieved Level 2 in all subjects at KS1 and is targeted for Level 4 in all subjects at KS2. He has a particular interest in Art.

Joe has thrived in his final year. We feel he has responded very positively to the greater expectations that have been placed upon him and that he will continue to thrive in a school that has a strong emphasis on high expectations.

Joe's peer group

Joe has a number of close friends in the village. As one of the older children in his class, he has tended to gravitate to children in the year above. Most of his friends are already attending Blankshire High School and he has set his heart on joining them there. About half of his current year are also due to attend the school and have been offered places, including his closest friend, Bob. This is a tight knit group and it will be very hard on Joe to be separated from them.

Joe's interests

Joe is an enthusiastic musician and is currently studying for his Royal Schools of Music grades. He has reached Grade 1 (merit) in flute and Grade 2 in euphonium. One of the attractions of Blankshire High School is the great emphasis it puts on music and drama. Joe performed with some gusto at his recent school play and greatly enjoyed it. He was particularly keen to see the drama facilities at the school on the open day and was very impressed by what he saw.

Like most 11-year-old boys he was also very keen to see the sports facilities the school has to offer. He is also an avid footballer and plays regularly for the village team. A statement from one of the team's coaches is attached. He is keen to learn to play rugby, and like most schoolboys, idolises Johnny Wilkinson.

Joe's needs

While Joe is an above-average child who is capable of producing very good work, he has allowed himself at times to be distracted. As we have now found out, part of that problem was due to him being the victim of bullying.

We also feel that while Little Snoring Primary School has catered extremely well for his pastoral and social needs, the school has not always been quite so good at catering for his educational development.

However, we are very happy with his final year at the school. He has responded very well to the differing expectations put on him in Year 6 by his teacher who engenders in her pupils a sense of self-discipline and personal achievement. This has been arguably his most successful academic year, and in terms of his own personal development unquestionably his best year at the school.

We are looking for a school that will build on this; one that sets and expects high standards, one that engenders good attitudes to work in its pupils. The 2003 Ofsted report for Blankshire High said: 'Standards are high in many subjects and continue to rise because pupils are generally well taught and have good attitudes to their work.'

Having visited Blankshire, the school to which Joe has been offered a place, and a third school, and having read their respective Ofsted reports and spoken to parents and children at all three schools, we passionately believe that Blankshire is the right place for Joe.

We believe that the very strong ethos the school puts on self-discipline and the very high expectations it has of its pupils, combined with the closeness of a smaller school in which he will not be 'just another Year 7', but known by the staff as an individual, is just the right environment in which Joe will thrive.

We are worried that if Joe attends his chosen school he will be subject to continued bullying
Unfortunately Joe's time at Little Snoring has been marred by incidents of psychological bullying and intimidation that have only recently come to light. The school has now taken steps to deal with this by separating Joe from the other child. He has responded well. However, in a small primary such as Little Snoring it is impossible to keep them completely apart. A letter from Mrs A Headteacher, the Headteacher, is attached.

The other child will be going to the school to which Joe has a place. We have approached Joe's current school to ask them to ensure that should this appeal be unsuccessful, that Joe is not put in the same group as this boy. However, given the small number of boys in Joe's current year group who will be going to this school, it is inevitable that the two will cross. Furthermore Joe and this boy will be forced to travel on the school bus together.

This boy has an older brother at the school and Joe is greatly worried that other older boys at the school will pick on him.

It is not our intention to denigrate the school that has offered Joe a place. It is a good school with many strengths, but it does not share the same values on discipline that are to be found at Blankshire and we are greatly concerned that the climate is less well controlled.

Their 2001 Ofsted report says, 'The main shortcomings are inadequate management of pupils' poor behaviour...' It goes on to say, 'Parents' concerns about behaviour and staffing are justified to some extent.' It also highlights one particular area of concern that we have: '... instances of foul language and insensitivity between pupils were seen. Many of these go unchecked, partly because there are few staff on duty in corridors at these times, and also because not all staff share consistently high expectations of pupils' conduct or dress.'

This contrasts starkly with Blankshire's attitudes and in particular, as reported to us by parents at the school, its very effective anti-bullying procedures.

Glossary

Admission round The period each year when parents are asked to apply to schools.

Admission authority The authority with the responsibility for setting the admission criteria. For most schools (VC and Community) it is the Local Authority (see below). However, it can delegate the authority down to the individual schools' governing bodies. For many schools with a religious character, and some other schools, the admission authority will be the school's governing body (VA and Foundation Schools).

Admission criteria The set of prioritised rules that will determine which pupils will be admitted to a school in the event of over-subscription. The admission authority draws up the admission criteria. They must by law be fair and objective and must be published annually in prospectuses and by local authorities in a prospectus explaining admissions at all schools in an area.

Banding Also known as streaming or setting. It describes the grouping of pupils for specific purposes. Usually it implies banding by ability.

Bilateral school Maintained school with two admission streams, one of which is selective. Bilateral schools may not keep open places in the selective stream if they are unable to find enough suitably qualified pupils.

Catchment area Some admission authorities give priority to children who live in an area around the school. The area is known as the catchment area. Sometimes known as a Priority Admissions Area.

Community school State schools in England and Wales that are wholly owned and maintained by the Local Authority. The Local Authority is the admission authority: it has main responsibility for deciding arrangements for admitting pupils (although some LAs have delegated the responsibility to the school's governing body).

Exclusion The suspension or expulsion of a pupil from school for disciplinary reasons. Rights of appeal are limited for parents of twice-excluded children.

Feeder school The informal title often given to primary schools that provide pupils to a specific secondary school. Also applied to secondary schools that send students to a particular sixth form college. Some admission authorities give priority to feeder schools.

Foundation school Type of state school which is run by the local authority but which has more freedom than community schools to manage the school and decide on its own admissions. At foundation schools, the governing body is the employer and the admission authority. The school's land and buildings are either owned by the governing body or by a charitable foundation.

Foundation stage The first stage of primary education covering children in the academic year of their fifth birthday.

Governing body The group of elected and appointed members at every school with responsibility for the management and school budget. Some governing bodies have responsibility for setting admission policies and arranging appeals.

Grammar school Schools that select all or almost all of their pupils by reference to academic ability.

Independent appeal panel The panel to which parents appeal against decisions made on areas such as admissions and exclusions. The admission authority is responsible for constituting an independent appeal panel, but the panel itself is independent in law. The decision of the panel is binding and can be challenged only by judicial review (all parties) or by complaining to the Local Government Ombudsman (parents only).

Indicated admission number (IAN) The calculated capacity of the school for a particular year group, determined by dividing the school's net capacity by the number of year groups. A school's published admission number (PAN) should be equal to or greater than the IAN. A school that wishes to set a PAN lower than the IAN must go through a period of consultation.

Infant class size prejudice Admission to a Key Stage 1 class which would require the admission authority to take 'qualifying measures' to comply with the limit of 30 pupils per class, and where these measures would cause prejudice to the school either in the year of admission or in a future school year.

Key Stage 1 (KS1) Children in Yrs 1 and 2 (Ages 5–7)

Key Stage 2 (KS2) Children in Yrs 3, 4, 5 and 6 (Ages 7–11)

Key Stage 3 (KS3) Children in Yrs 7, 8 and 9 (Ages 11–14)

Key Stage 4 (KS4) Children in Yrs 10 and 11 (Ages 14–17)

Local Authority (LA) The local government body responsible for setting and financing education policy. Previously, and often still, referred to as the Local Education Authority.

Local Government Ombudsman The statutory body that investigates complaints of injustice arising from maladministration by an appeal panel. Parents may appeal to the Ombudsman if they feel that their case has been handled unjustly (maladministration), but not simply if they disagree with the outcome.

Mainstream school Belonging or relating to the mainstream in accordance with what is 'normal' or 'standard', as opposed to a 'Special School'.

Maintained schools A term for all state schools.

Maladministration There is no legal definition, but generally it applies to a panel that has not acted reasonably in accordance with the law, its own policies and generally accepted standards of local administration.

Middle school A middle school has pupils from KS2 and KS3. Depending on the age balance of those pupils, the school can be deemed primary or secondary.

Ofsted report Report by an official body that regularly inspects all mainly or wholly state-funded schools in England. Ofsted inspectors produce education reports which are meant to improve standards of achievement and quality of education, provide public reporting and informed independent advice.

Parent Apart from the normal definition, in educational terms the term 'parent' includes any person who is not a natural parent of the child but who has parental responsibility for him or her; any person who has care of the child.

Performance tables The Department for Education and Skills publishes comparative secondary and 16–18 performance tables each year. The tables report achievements in public examinations and vocational qualifications in secondary schools and Further Education sector colleges. Primary school performance tables are published by local education authorities and report the achievements of pupils at the end of Key Stage 2.

Phase Refers to the broad grouping of children at a school. Categories include: nursery, infant, junior, primary, middle deemed primary, middle deemed secondary, secondary, upper, sixth form.

Presenting officer The person appointed by the admission authority to present the case at the independent appeal. For Community and VC schools the presenting officer will usually be an LA official, although the Headteacher will sometimes take the role. In the case of VA and Foundation schools it is usually a governor, often the chair of the admission committee, who presents the case.

Prospectus A brochure containing useful facts and figures, which the governing body must publish each year for parents and prospective parents. Ministers set minimum requirements for content, so that parents can make comparisons between different schools. Copies will be available at the school for reference or are free of charge to parents on request.

Published admission number (PAN) The number of pupils the school will admit. A school must admit up to the PAN. Admission criteria will only be applied if the number of applicants exceeds the PAN.

Qualifying measures Steps taken by a primary or infant school in the event of having a class of more than 30 children. These steps may include recruiting additional staff.

Special educational needs (SEN) This denotes any child who has been identified as having some form of additional educational need. These children receive additional support either from within the school, or from outside agencies. Note that more able children (also known as 'talented and gifted' children) are not defined as having special educational needs.

Special school Maintained schools in England and Wales that are provided by local education authorities for certain children with special educational needs. Application to such schools, and appeals against applications, are dealt with differently from applications to mainstream schools.

Specialist school A school with a specialism in one or more prescribed subjects and which allows the admission arrangements for the school to give priority to up to 10% of pupils who can demonstrate an aptitude in the relevant subject. There are five subjects: physical education or sport or one or more sports; the performing arts or one or more of those arts; the visual arts or one or more of those arts; modern foreign languages or any such language; design and technology and information technology. An admission authority cannot leave places unfilled if there are not enough pupils to fill the proportion of selective aptitude places.

Standard number The old system used to calculate the number of places at a school. Has now been replaced by the published admission number, although the term is still widely used. Also called the number intended to admit (NIA).

Statement of special educational needs These statements describe any learning difficulties which pupils have, and specify the extra help or equipment they need. Around 3% of school pupils nationally have statements. Sometimes known just as a 'statement'.

Voluntary Aided school (VA school) Schools in England and Wales that are maintained by the LA, with a foundation (generally religious) that appoints most of the governing body. The Local Authority is the admission authority. (See also governing body.)

Voluntary Controlled school (VC school) Schools in England and Wales that are maintained by the LA, with a foundation (generally religious) that appoints most, but not all, of the governing body. The Local Authority is the admission authority, although in some cases it can devolve responsibility to the governing body. (See also governing body; Local Authority.)

Waiting list If an admission authority keeps a waiting list, it must include details of the criteria by which children will be admitted off the waiting list. These must be clear, fair and objective and not simply depend on the date of application.

Year group The way the years are divided in English schools, from nursery through to sixth form. Foundation year: 4/5-year-olds; Year 1, 5/6-year-olds; Year 2: 6/7-year-olds; Year 3: 7/8-year-olds; Year 4: 8/9-year-olds; Year 5: 9/10-year-olds; Year 6: 10/11-year-olds; Year 7: 11/12-year-olds; Year 8: 12/13-year-olds; Year 9: 13/14-year-olds; Year 10: 14/15-year-olds; Year 11: 15/16-year-olds; Year 12: 16/17-year-olds; Year 13: 17/18-year-olds.